An atlas
of typeforms

An atlas
of typeforms

James Sutton and Alan Bartram

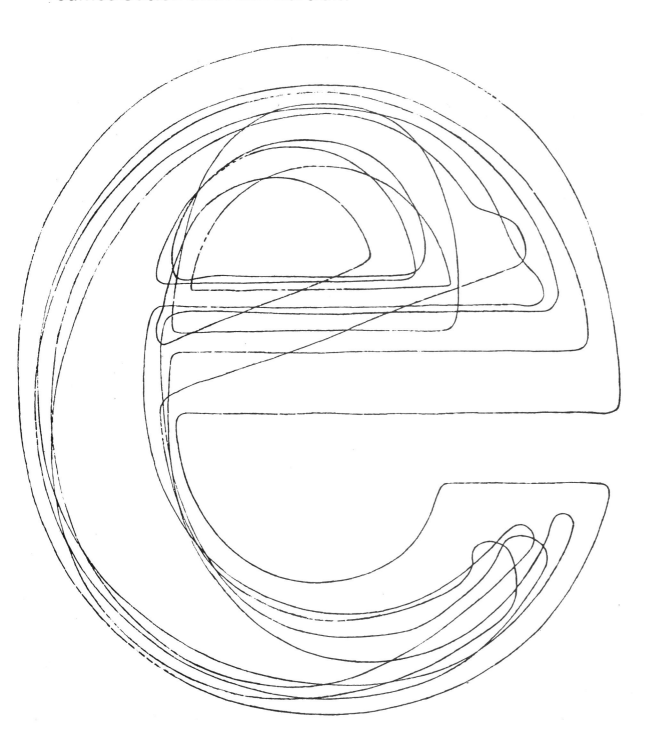

CHARTWELL
BOOKS, INC.

Contents

Authors' note

**This book contains many examples of type
specimens which have been deliberately enlarged.
These are intended to facilitate the study and
comparison of their shapes and principal features.
Wherever possible these enlargements have been
taken from 30pt letters. Some types, however, are
not available in sizes larger than 14pt or even 9pt
and in these cases the largest available size has
been used as a basis. The heavier weight of small
sizes and the distortion caused by great enlargement produces a coarse and clumsy image. To
retouch would have been misleading as it would
virtually have meant redesigning the type for the
larger size, and so we have merely drawn
attention to enlargements from small originals
with this mark: ≣**

Note to the 1988 edition

An Atlas of Typeforms was first published in 1968, and is a
unique record of five centuries of metal type. Since the original
publication, the whole process of creating type has changed.
Redrawn for photocomposition and redrawn again for digital
setting, the type names stay the same, but shapes and sizes
have altered. The last twenty years have seen more
technological development to the printing process than the
previous five centuries.

An Atlas of Typeforms is today not a working tool, but a classic
record of metal type design.

This note, and the new imprint and copyright information
below, are set with the aid of current technology, and are
presented in 7/8½pt Compugraphic 8600 Univers Medium,
Italic and Bold.

Published by
CHARTWELL BOOKS INC.
A Division of **BOOK SALES, INC.**
110 Enterprise Avenue
Secaucus, New Jersey 07094

Copyright © 1968 Percy Lund, Humphries & Co Ltd.
Designed by Alan Bartram

ISBN 1-55521-340-5

Printed and bound in Portugal by Printer Portuguesa Industria Grafica.

Acknowledgments

For their advice and assistance during the preparation of
the Atlas, the authors wish to record their gratitude to :
John Dreyfus and Alan Jones (The Monotype
Corporation) ; James Mosley (St Bride Printing Library) ;
Walter Tracy (Linotype & Machinery Ltd) ; Dr Michael
Twyman (University of Reading) ; John Ward-Perkins
(The British School at Rome) ; Berthold Wolpe (Faber &
Faber) ; and Herbert Spencer. Naturally, however, any
opinions expressed, and any errors or omissions, are
entirely the responsibility of the authors.

The authors and publishers wish to thank the following
for permission to reproduce material in the Atlas : Barrow
in Furness Public Library ; Bibliothèque Nationale, Paris ;
British Museum, London ; Museum of English Rural Life,
University of Reading ; St Bride Printing Library, London ;
Stiftsbibliothek, St Gallen ; The Board of Trinity College,
Dublin ; Vatican Library, Rome ; Victoria and Albert
Museum, London.

The specimen text settings on the pull-out at the end of
the Atlas make use of an extract from *Pnin* by Vladimir
Nabokov, by courtesy of the publishers, Doubleday &
Company Inc, New York and William Heinemann Ltd,
London.

Finally, the authors and publishers wish to express
their grateful thanks to all those type-founders and printers
listed below who have generously contributed specimens
of typefaces and information about them. Without their
help, this Atlas of Typeforms would not have been
possible.

American Type Founders Company, Inc
Elizabeth, NJ

NV Lettergieterij en Machinehandel
voorheen N. Tetterode-Nederland
Amsterdam

Bauersche Giesserei
Frankfurt/Main

H. Berthold Messinglinienfabrik und Schriftgiesserei AG
Berlin

Cambridge University Press

Deberny & Peignot
Paris

Joh. Enschedé en Zonen
Haarlem

Haas'sche Schriftgiesserei AG
Münchenstein BL, Switzerland

Harris-Intertype Gmbh
Berlin

Linotype & Machinery Limited
Altrincham

Linotype Gmbh
Frankfurt/Main

London Transport

Ludlow Typograph Company
Chicago

Ludwig & Mayer
Frankfurt/Main

Mergenthaler Linotype Inc
Brooklyn, NY

The Monotype Corporation Limited
London

Società Nebiolo
Turin

Fonderie Olive
Marseilles

University Press
Oxford

The Shenval Press Ltd
Harlow

D. Stempel AG
Frankfurt/Main

Stephenson Blake & Company Ltd
Sheffield

Steven Shanks & Sons Limited
London

Waterlow & Sons Limited
London

C. E. Weber Schriftgiesserei
Stuttgart

William Morris wrote of Nicholas Jenson's Roman : 'This type I studied with much care, getting it photographed to a big scale, and drawing it over many times before I began designing my own letter.'

This atlas is an attempt to show by illustration, rather than by explaining in words, the main changes in type forms over 500 years of printing. We have enlarged many of the most important types in the history of printing so that their shapes can be seen clearly and compared. We also show, only slightly reduced, an original use of the type, which further demonstrates its qualities ; then follow enlarged letters and full alphabets derived from or in the manner of the same historical original.

We have used the broadly chronological headings of Old Face, Transitional, Modern, etc, rather than more sophisticated systems whose virtues are still being debated. Many types today have no very clear ancestry as under modern conditions the use of old type face designs is only possible after drastic revision ; but when learning about types the authors found it helpful to look at the designs of the past in their historical setting. There seemed to be a continuity in the changes in letter forms which made them easier to understand and identify, and comparison with modern faces gave a useful insight into their nature. Equally important influences on the shapes of printed letters are the ways in which the type is cast, and the techniques of printing. Books on these subjects and a short list of type histories will be found in the bibliography at the end of the atlas.

The basic process of founding type is the same whether it is done by hand or by machine. A punch, consisting of a relief letter, reversed left to right, is struck into a slab of softer metal to produce a matrix into which is poured the molten type metal. This is an exact and intricate process : it is partly engineering and partly engraving, and is very different from writing, drawing or carving letters. Gutenberg was a goldsmith, and the greatest of his successors were engravers interested in the technique of printing as much as with the layout of books. In this atlas we focus attention on the shapes of the letters, but however beautiful or impressive these may be in themselves, their success entirely depends on how well they make up into words : a matter of technical skill as much as of aesthetic judgement.

Punches were cut by hand until the American invention of the punch cutting machine in the 1890's. Now a pantograph traces the outline of a large drawn letter and automatically cuts a punch to the required reduction. This makes for much greater control and accuracy, and allows the designer to dispense with the craft of the metal engraver. However, in the past, many of the finest typefaces were designed and cut by artists who were also masters of printing techniques. From Jenson to Bodoni we see typography that demonstrates this unity of design and production, only possible in a small organisation, but no longer commercially practicable in twentieth-century conditions. Not that the general run of printed material is poor, but it obviously must be judged by different criteria, and it lacks the special, sometimes precious, qualities of private press work.

Machine setting for large-scale production does not necessarily make for lower standards. Indeed, if carefully designed it can equal hand-set work. Some limitations in typeforms and in design are, however, inherent in the various composing machine systems currently in use. Of these the Linotype and a closely similar machine the Intertype combine the casting of type with the task of composing it into words. A keyboard selects matrices (maximum composition size 48pt) and adjustable spaces, which are forced between words to space the line out to its full measure. This justified line is then cast as a solid metal bar. The machine is designed in such a way that italics and bolds are generally the same width as romans, and letters cannot be arranged to overhang one another. Italics thus appear too wide in form or too loosely fitting together, and bolds too narrow or light in weight. Sometimes, however, special italic matrices are struck in the correct condensed form.

Monotype machines cast characters singly and will compose text in up to 14pt to almost twice the length of a line set by Linotype (sixty picas as opposed to thirty-six). The range of typefaces available is very large and although there are certain limitations on the fit of letters together, in practice these are very slight design restrictions. Italics and bolds can appear in their visually appropriate widths, and overhanging (kerning) is possible ; and the system allows for more of the finer points of letter design and more typographical freedom.

The Ludlow system is semi-mechanized : the compositor sets up matrices and spaces by hand from which a line of type is cast. Sizes from 4pt to 144pt are available and it is possible to set up to twice the measure possible on Monotype machines. It is especially useful for display composition but has the same typographic limitations as Linotype.

In general, Linotype and Intertype are most used for newspapers and books, Ludlow for newspapers and general display, and Monotype for all kinds of printing, but less for newspapers. All four systems operate internationally, though some Linotype and Intertype faces available in Germany or America, for example, are not obtainable in England and cannot be adapted to English machines. All Monotype faces are theoretically available in all countries. Foreign founders' types for hand-setting can also be imported through their agents, although English and American sizes differ from European standards. Founders' type-metal, having to withstand continual re-use, is harder than that of machine-set type which is melted down after each job. Type at the end of a very long run may print a coarser letter, and fine serifs or thin strokes may break.

The choice of a good typeform must be governed by many considerations such as availability, compatibility with the paper and printing process, as well as visual effect. Unfamiliar or eccentric forms can succeed in display but are fatal in text, where the line should flow without interruption, though each character must be impossible to confuse with another. The contrast between thick and thin strokes should be slighter in text faces : oblique shading for thick strokes emphasizes the differences in letterforms and helps the flow of reading. Too great a contrast gives a brilliant effect but tends to dazzle. Capitals should not be obtrusive in weight or in relation to height of ascenders. The design of a face should be modified carefully for different sizes. Monotype faces are redrawn every other size, and in some series 6pt is very different from 10pt, while retaining the same basic character. Faces for film-setting are far less delicately considered ; in some cases one design serves for all sizes, though in theory this technique offers fewest limitations of all to subtleties of design and setting.

The appearance of type is affected as much by the way it is used as by its design. Nearly all were designed for the letterpress process : pressing inked metal against paper. The ink is squeezed to the outer edge of the letter giving a hard sharp image. Over-inking produces ink-squash which enlarges and distorts the printed form. The texture of the paper and the weight and fine detail of the type must be carefully chosen and understood for a perfect impression.

In offset-lithography no ink-squash takes place, but until recently a soft image was a common fault. Improved technique now makes a crisp black image possible. Typeforms are radically affected by printing techniques, and modern machinery would literally make light of many old designs. Until this century all books were printed on dampened paper, the type impressed into the soft surface. The paper was then dried and rolled between hot cylinders. Such techniques are now too slow and costly, and modern paper is harder and smoother and able to take a light, rapid, 'kiss' impression.

These are a few of many factors affecting the shapes of typeforms ; this book attempts to trace their origins and evolution not only during recent centuries, but by way of medieval writing from the script of Charlemagne and by way of Renaissance calligraphy from the first-century inscriptions of Imperial Rome.

Roman capital letters first achieved the forms we know today about AD 100. The inscriptions carved at the time of the emperors still exist, and the shapes of the letters have been copied and re-copied through the centuries by scribes and architects, engravers and type-designers.

At their most formal they are based on very simple geometric shapes, symbols for the sounds in a language. And each letter is successful as a symbol because its shape is hard to confuse with the others and is easy to memorize.

The alphabet became internationally recognized as a system of communication in many languages and thus the shapes became fixed. To alter them would have been to destroy their effectiveness. But the exact shapes of the Roman capitals are elusive, with many variations on the geometric substructure. These freely drawn lines which do not correspond to the arc of a circle or a perfect straight edge, yet are highly controlled, give the alphabet its particular quality of strength and poise.

Apart from their underlying geometry their shapes were formed by the way they were drawn on the stone. They were first marked out with a broad reed pen or sign-writer's brush cut square at the tip, and thus acquired their thick and thin strokes. Then they were cut into the stone with a sharp chisel. This gave them disciplined curves and angles and determined the form of their stroke endings. These serifs occur naturally through carving, but have to be artificially built up when they are drawn with a pen.

Roman inscriptional capitals have great authority due to their geometry and stone-carved precision. They have a subtle rhythmic tension because they are also written or calligraphic forms. Unlike most modern signwriters and monumental masons, Roman letter cutters had the skill of

great virtuosi. Their finest work demonstrates the essential qualities of lettering : immediate recognition of form and also the possibility of varying the arrangement and style of lettering for different purposes, without loss of meaning : the shapes are formal and standardized, but also virile and flexible.

Capitals carved in marble : the originals are three inches high. Via Appia Antica, Rome.
Photo: James Mosley

Roman letters are best known from the alphabet used for the Trajan inscription. This merits the closest study for the austere quality of its letter forms and the formal architectural authority of its spacing and arrangement on the stone. The upper lines of the text have larger letters to give an even appearance from the ground. At the same time the letters have a mysterious delicacy and buoyancy. This inscription has profoundly influenced typography and type-design.

But carved Roman capitals varied greatly in style.

Opposite, a Roman bold and a Roman sans of the classical era are compared with Trajan lettering. Other inscriptions show broad forms with decorated serifs or condensed script-like shapes known as Rustics. Many were painted as well as incised, and some, as the second example opposite, were metal filled.

Obviously the effect of white marble in the Italian sun has a great influence on the design of these inscriptions. Much of their delicacy and sparkle would be lost on soft stone in a grey climate.

Inscription on the base of Trajan's Column in the Forum, Rome c. AD 114. *Photo: James Mosley*

If the monumental inscriptions fixed the shapes of the Roman alphabet, informal written letters of the same date show how their forms break down into minuscules, with strokes above and below the line. An A is made from three separate straight lines but if the pen is kept on the paper the form changes to *A* and when written quickly to *a*. A bill or a laundry list scribbled on papyrus or wax in the first century looks surprisingly like modern handwriting, even though the actual letterforms are unfamiliar and almost illegible.

Many years passed before these changes were incorporated in serious writing. However, even in examples of the great formal scripts used for books between the first and eighth centuries, some minuscule shapes begin to appear. The written letters nearest to the inscriptional capitals are called Quadrata or Square Capitals. They retain a stately geometry and must have been slow to write.

Rustics, a second formal book script, have slightly condensed letter forms, more suitable to calligraphy. The line is broken by a few large letters, the u is invented (a typical pen-form), and the crossbar of the A disappears. Rustics are less sombre and easier to read than Quadrata, though they have no spaces between the words.

Roman Uncials, the book script used for many early Christian documents, show some important changes in the development of lower case. The ascending and descending strokes have become an important feature of the alphabet and, as a result, words can be recognized more easily.

By AD 700 many regional styles of book script were in use in Europe, as well as many informal hands. The Book of Kells, one of the most magnificent books ever produced, was written in the regional style current in the British Isles known as Anglo-Irish Half Uncials. The text is written in a fully formed minuscule alphabet; the ascenders and descenders properly form parts of letters and are no longer accidental flourishes. The serifs are strong pen-made shapes, and not artificial constructions harking back to capital letters.

Square Capitals, Rustics and Uncials were still used for headings or for short lengths of text. By the end of the eighth century the strength and legibility of the Anglo-Irish script led Charlemagne to choose Alcuin of York to supervise the new imperial scriptorium at Tours. A new style of writing was needed to replace the current regional styles in order to give the Emperor's documents international authority and clarity, just as a firm today might have a house style designed to give its printed matter unity and a clear identity.

The new script, known as Carolingian minuscules, was developed at Tours and elsewhere in Europe from the Anglo-Irish Half Uncial and the local French book hand known as Merovingian. From it grew the great book hands of the Middle Ages which, like the arches in medieval architecture, began round and massive and later became delicate and pointed.

1. Square Caps. Virgil, fourth–fifth century.
Stiftsbibliothek, St Gallen.
Slowly read and slowly written geometric forms. No
spaces separate words or sentences. L and F are slightly
taller than the other letters. Arrangement and spacing are
inscriptional, but the pen forms the thicks and thins and
also the serifs.

2. Rustics. Virgil, fourth–fifth century.
Vatican Library, Rome.
A genuine pen form ; condensed, rhythmic and flowing, it
makes a rich texture on the page. Though quicker to write
it is still hard to read. The crossbar of the A has
disappeared.

3. Rustics. Prudentius : Hymns, fifth century.
Bibliothèque Nationale, Paris.
A more freely written example of Rustic script. The larger
spaces between lines and letters make the text much
easier to read.

4. Uncials. Gospels, sixth–seventh century.
British Museum, London.
Though nearer to Square Caps than to Rustics in their
formality and grandeur, these Uncials show many signs of
the breakdown of capital letters. A D E F M P U are
now lower-case forms and the ascending and
descending strokes make the page less formal and the
words more legible.

5. Uncials. Gospel of St Matthew, eighth century.
Bibliothèque Nationale, Paris.
A very finely written example. The pen is held very
straight, giving emphasis to the vertical strokes. There is
some slight and irregular word spacing.

6. Uncials. St Cyprian : Letters, fourth–fifth century.
Vatican Library, Rome.
An early example of Uncials showing the appearance of
lower-case forms, in a rich, black calligraphic texture.

7. Half Uncials. St Hilarius : de Trinitate, c. AD 500.
Vatican Library, Rome.
Here the new lower-case forms predominate, and the
whole look of the page becomes irregular and informal.
In spite of very little word separation, the page is more
legible, and the long ascenders which drive the lines
apart produce a unified but lighter texture on the page.

8. Half Uncials. Manuscript from Southern Italy,
sixth century. Vatican Library, Rome.
A freely written script in which the surviving cap forms
halt the flow of the calligraphy. Note various treatments of
stroke endings.

9. Anglo-Irish Half Uncial. Book of Kells : Latin Gospels,
seventh century. Trinity College Library, Dublin.
A genuine script with established lower-case forms of the
greatest nobility and grandeur. Note word separation,
serifs and powerful rhythm of strokes.

10. Carolingian. Alcuin Bible written at Tours, ninth
century. British Museum, London.
This light, legible, mobile script, developed in
Charlemagne's scriptorium, was imitated by Renaissance
scribes and thus became the model for the first roman
lower-case printing type.

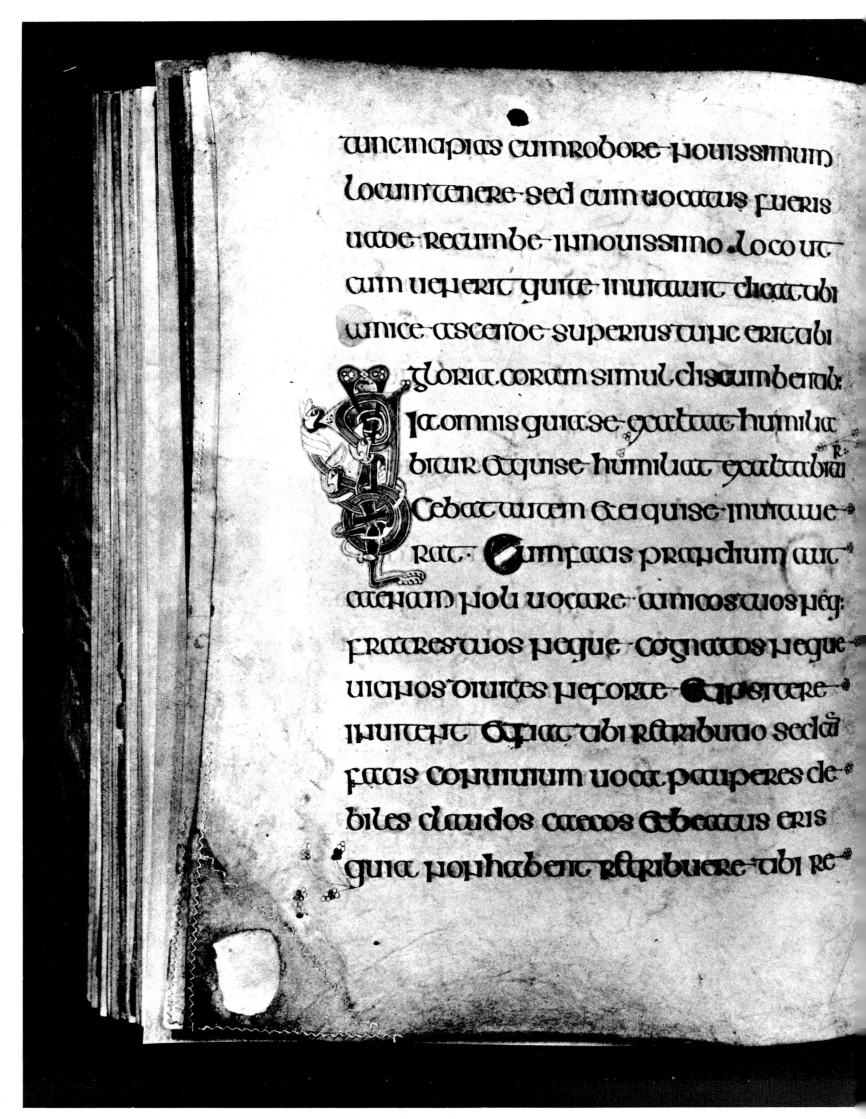

tribuetur enim tibi in resurrectione ius-
torum · Hec · cum audiss & quidam
desimul discumbentibus dixit illi be-
atus qui manducabit panem in regno di
Ipse dixit ei homo quidam fecit
caenam magnam & uocauit mul
tos & misit seruum suum ad horam
caenae dicere inuitatis ut uenirent
quia iam parata sunt omnia
coeperunt simul omnes excusare
primus dixit ei uillam emi & necesse
se+ habeo exire & uidere illam rogo
te habe me excusatum Alter
dixit iuga bouum emi quinque
eo probare illa & ideo uenire non
possum rogo te habe me excusatum
& alius dixit uxorem duxi & ideo

The scripts on page 10 show early manuscripts in the most formal styles from Square Caps to Uncials. They can be compared with those on page 11 which show the growth of a more flowing calligraphic tradition, which culminated in the general adoption of Carolingian.

During the Middle Ages two main characteristics can again be recognized, the round, vigorous shapes on this page, and the more sombre condensed forms on the page opposite, which were to be further narrowed, pointed and formalized during the thirteenth and fourteenth centuries, particularly in northern Europe. And when Gutenberg cut his type, it was upon Textura, a particularly grand and austere pointed gothic book script, that he based his design.

1. Psalter, southern England, AD 975.
British Museum, London.
2. Benedictional, eleventh century. 'Neo-Carolingian'.
British Museum, London.
3. Homilies, Italy, early twelfth century.
British Museum, London.

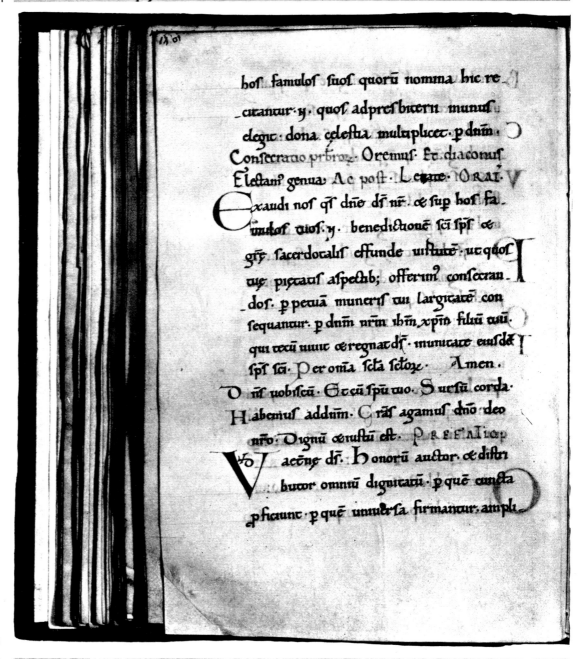

4. Pontifical, England, twelfth century.
British Museum, London.
This manuscript is particularly interesting apart from its
magnificence as an object in itself. The serifs recall those
of The Book of Kells, but the condensed forms and heavy,
black, vertical strokes look ahead to late gothic
calligraphy.

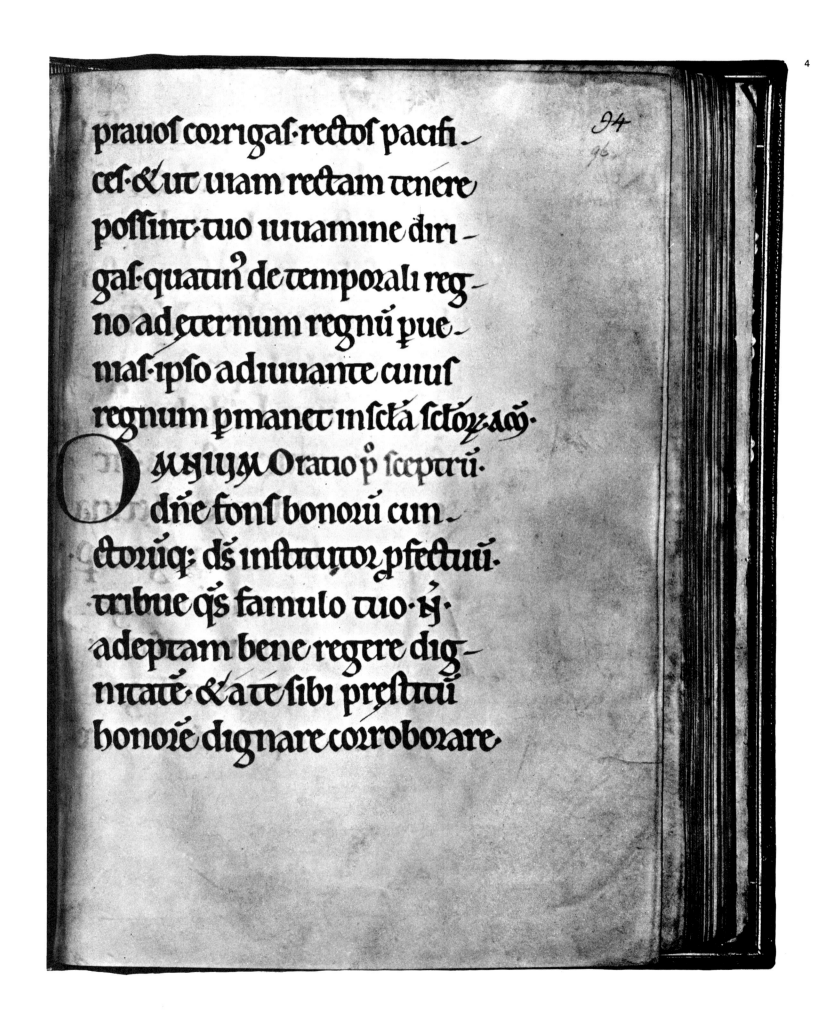

adducti : & singulari relligione & precipua
deuotione prediti pie admodum credideru
nt / nihil enim aliud quicquam ei nature /
quam tam pulchram tam ingeniosam et
tam sapientem ac tam opulentam tam di
gnam & tam potentem postremo tam feli
cem & tam beatam constituerat ad totam
& undique absolutam perfectionem suam
de esse putabatur : nisi ut ea per admixtion
em cum ipsa diuinitate non solum coniuncta
in illa christi persona cum diuina sed etiam
ut cum diuina natura una & sola efficeret
ac per hunc modum unica facta fuisse uide
retur : quod neq; angelis neq; ulli alie creatu
re nisi homini dumtaxat ad admirabilem
quandam humane nature dignitatem et
ad incredibilem quoque eius ipsius excellen
tiam datum concessum & attributum esse
nouimus .

AD EVNDEM EIVSDEM LIBER

QVARTVS INCIPIT. FELICITER .

ACTENVS CVNCTA
que ad singularem quandam
& precipuam dignitatem &
excellentiam hominis uel ma
xime spectare & pertinere ui
debantur . quantum paruu
la ingenii nostri facultas permittere opera
ri ue poterat . tribus precedentibus libris spa
rsim ac diffuse claro quodam & aperto ser
mone congessimus . Itaque oportunum qu
oddam & accommodatum uenisse & occur
risse tempus non iniuria existimauimus
Vt ultimas huic operi manus imponeremus quod
profecto iam fecissemus nisi nostra interesse pu
taremus ut ea refelleremus . que a pluribus pri
scis nouellisq; auctoribus . uel de laudatione et
bono mortis uel de miseria humane uite scrip
ta fuisse intelligebamus : quoniam ea illis á no
bis antea tractatis aliquatenus repugnare a
nimaduertebamus . Sed in hac nostra predic
tarum uelut friuolarum ac falsarum opinio
num confutatione ordine quodam uti consti
tuimus . ut res ipsa grauius seueriusq; tracte
tur . Primo namq; ad ea que de fragilitate hu

1

Textura was one of the last monuments of the Middle
Ages ; in Italy, however, the Renaissance had awakened a
new demand for the writings of classical authors. Before
the invention of printing these were transcribed from old
manuscripts of the twelfth century written in late
Carolingian minuscules. The fifteenth-century scribes
mistook this for the book hand of Rome and enthusiasti-
cally modelled their own script upon Carolingian. In their
writing we at once recognize the model on which the
first roman types were based. The letters are round, open,
clear, sane and secular, and are known as Humanistic
minuscules. In contrast to the awesome blackness of
Textura, with its close-packed vertical strokes of similar
shape, the Italian manuscript books are light and graceful,
with plenty of white space between the words and lines.
Even more important, the letters themselves are
perfectly distinct shapes, well formed and regular, with
the minuscule serifs carefully shaped to correspond with
those of the capital letters. These serifs are not easily
made by the pen, and owe their shape to the imitation of
serifs on carved roman capitals.

The cursive script developed during the fifteenth
century in Florence and in the Papal Chancery at Rome
are the principal models of italic type ; the sixteenth-
century example on the right shows an effective use of
roman and cursive and also the interaction of writing and
printing. The scribe seems to be composing separate
minuscules into words, and few are joined even in the
cursive.

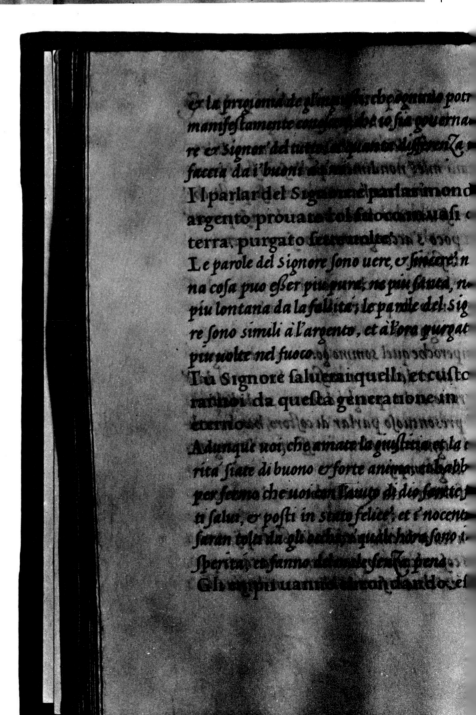

1. De dignitate et excellentia Hominis (written by Gherado del Ciriagio). Florence, 1454. British Museum, London.
2. Hours of Bonaparte Ghislieri of Bologna (writing attributed to Pierantonio Sallando), 1500. British Museum, London.
3. Marcantonio Flaminio. La Paraphrasi, sixteenth century. British Museum, London.

suauitatem odoris. Tu autem
domine miserere nostri. R̅
Deo gratias: R̅ Felix namque
es sacra uirgo maria et omni
laude dignissima. Quia ex te
ortus est sol iusticie. Christus
deus noster. V. Ora pro popu
lo interueni pro clero: interce
de pro deuoto femineo sexu
sentiant omnes tuum iuuame
quicunq̄ celebrant tuam san
ctam commemorationem
Quia ex te ortus est sol

ster. Canticum scorum am
brosij et Augustini.
E deum laudamus: te
dominum confitemur.
e eternum patrem omnis
terra ueneratur.
ibi omnes angeli: tibi celi
et uniuerse potestates:
ibi cherubin et seraphin
i cessabili uoce proclamant
anctus Sanctus San
ctus dn̄s deus sabaoth
leni sunt celi et terra: r

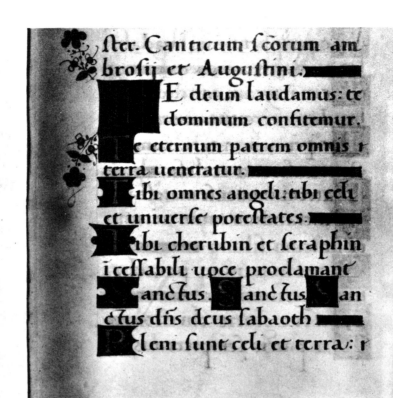

2

3

do essaltati i piú uili de i figliuoli de
gli huomini.
Quando gli huomini ingiusti et uitiosi sono
signori, all'hora i ribaldi pigliano forza, e
licentiosamente fanno del male; et offendono
quelli che con fede, et con giustitia uiuono.
꿈 SOPRA IL SALMO
XIIJ.
Questo sant'huomo gia uenuto quasi al me=
ɔ per le molte, et continoue calamita, ha com
passion di se stesso, et con la mente domanda
aiuto di dio.
꿈 AL VENCITORE salmo
XIIJ.
nfino à quanto Signore ti domenti=
i di me in perpetouo? infino a quã
ascondi la faccia tua da me?
Signore infin'à quanto lasci tu in tante mise=
colui, che ti prega? infin'à quanto uuoi tu,
e duri lo sdegno tuo contro di me, et il tuo nõ tu
e de la mia salute?
nfino à quanto porro'io consigli ne'

The first printers

The series of technical inventions and developments made by Gutenberg at Mainz around 1440 were of such colossal importance in shaping the modern world that he is justly recognized as one of the greatest figures of the Renaissance. Prints had been taken from wood blocks many years earlier, but his invention of printing by movable, interchangeable, re-usable type was the foundation of the modern printing industry, and his discoveries and methods were only superseded in the early nineteenth century. By trade a goldsmith, his work was of the highest technical standard and his ingenuity in the many aspects of printing, and in particular book production, made his printed books the equal of the manuscripts they rivalled. The script he took as his model for the forty-two-line Bible of 1455 was Textura, the most sombre and majestic script then current in northern Europe. It gives the page a noble authority, but its close-packed, heavy, vertical strokes and easily confused letter forms make words static and rigid and therefore hard to read. Five years later, for the Catholicon, he used a far less impressive type with weak characterless letterforms. But the text of the Catholicon was set in small type like a modern book and the shapes of the letters were round, open and legible.

1

2

Printing was brought to Italy, the artistic and commercial centre of the Renaissance, by Germans, and Gutenberg's typography throws its shadow over the early Roman types of the 1460's.

The 'colour' of type on the page, governed by the shapes of the letters and the spacing of the letters, words and lines, is a most important consideration in typography. The dark colour of these early printed books was much admired by William Morris in the 1890's and by many of his followers in the private press movement in England, and later in the USA and Germany. The standards which these amateur printers re-established, from a study of books printed before 1500, were taken up by the printing industry as a whole, though few books were produced commercially in the rather precious style of the private presses.

1. Lactanius : Opera. Sweynheym and Pannartz, Subiaco, 1465. British Museum, London.
Roman shapes expressed in gothic calligraphy, with pen-made forms dominating strokes and serifs of capitals and lower case. The letters are rather condensed in shape and set close, giving the page a dark appearance, relieved to some extent by spots of colour applied to the capitals by hand after printing.

2. Cicero : Letters. Sweynheim and Pannartz, Rome, 1470. British Museum, London.
On moving to Rome in 1467 the German printers cut a new type which had no gothic characteristics. It became known soon afterwards simply as roman type and was thus differentiated from gothic. It was imitated elsewhere in Italy and abroad. Though imperfect in design and roughly made it was recognized as a type of the new age.

3. Cicero : Letters. da Spira, Venice, 1469. British Museum, London.
The da Spira brothers were also Germans, but their version of 'roman' for their press in Venice is a great advance on the types of Sweynheym and Pannartz. Round and open, the type has a good fit with close and even letter spacing without cramping. The shapes are well drawn and well cut and produce an even, easily read page of text.

Below are shown two private press types. The first is *Golden*, designed by William Morris for the Kelmscott Press in 1890 ; the punches were cut by E. P. Prince, and the type was first used in Morris's *Golden Legend* in 1892 (see page 97). Beneath this is shown *Brook*, designed by Lucien Pissarro in 1903. Both these types are now in the possession of the Cambridge University Press.

ABCDEFGHIJKLMN
OPQRSTUVWXYZ
abcdefghijklmnopqrstuvwxyzæœ
fffiflffiffl&ÆŒ1234567890.,;:-!?'()

ABCDEFGHIJKLMN
OPQRSTUVWXYZ
abcdefghijklmnopqrstuvwxyzæœ
&ÆŒ1234567890.,;:-!?'()

Among the Venetian printers, however, the great merits of the new letter were not at once victorious; and although roman was thought appropriate for classical texts, gothic was used for liturgical, legal and vernacular works. The great printer Erhard Ratdolt uses both roman and gothic in the book shown on this page, and elsewhere he used the old letter in conjunction with the delicate borders and wide margins of Renaissance typography.

4. Eusebius. Erhard Ratdolt, Venice, 1483. Victoria and Albert Museum, London.

The finest version of the roman letter was cut by a contemporary of Ratdolt's at Venice, the Frenchman Nicholas Jenson. The enlarged letters shown below are from his roman type of 1470, which has been praised by experts down the centuries as no other type has been praised. It is also the design from which the first group of modern printing types is derived: the Venetians. Jenson's letters are finely cut, with a gradual change from thick to thin strokes. The serifs are strong and steeply sloped, those on the capitals have almost no brackets, while those in the lower case are almost only brackets. The M has serifs on

the inside and the e has a small eye with an oblique bar. These details are common to the Venetian family of typefaces. But even Jenson returned to gothic typography, though the two styles seem to us totally different in appearance and association: one, the dark, constricted, highly formalized expression of the Middle Ages: the other, an open, freely drawn product of the Renaissance.

4

From Nonius: Peripatetica. Nicholas Jenson, Venice, 1476

Nonius : Peripatetica. Nicholas Jenson, Venice, 1476.
Victoria and Albert Museum, London.
Black-letter heaviness, vertical stress and angular forms
found in late gothic script and early Italian types are
forgotten in the so-called white-letter roman of Nicholas
Jenson : the model taken by Morris for his Golden type in
1890, Cobden Sanderson for the Doves type of 1901 and

Bruce Rogers for Centaur in 1915. Jenson's grand
typography, the satisfactory fit of his letters into words
and the beautiful proportions of the letters themselves
show why he is admired above all Venetian printers and
type-cutters who were working during the fifteenth
century ; he raised the craft of printing to an art in its own
right.

Rumā ueteres māmam dixerūt. M. Cato li.de liberis educā.
Hifce māibus lacte fit nō uino eumna ppter eunos rumfe
propter rumā. i. prifco uocabulo māmam : a quo fubrimi
etiā nunc dicuntur agni.

Reiculas oues: aut ætate aut morbo graues . Marcus Cato libro de liberis educandis : Et ut in grege opilio minus ido-
neas oues remouere folet : quas reiculas appellat . Sæpe
enim unus puer petulans atq; impurus inquit gregem
pueror.

DE DICTIONIBVS AB. S.
LITTERA INCIPIENTIBVS.

SAltuatim bellicatim . Sifenna hiftoria-
rum libro primo : Nos una ætate in afia
& græcia gefta litteris iccirco continentia
mandauimus : ne bellicatim ac faltua-
tim fcribendo lectorum animos im-
pediremus.

Scapum. Varro in marco: Mihiq; diui-
tum ftilo noftro papyrino liuii fcapo fcapitio nouo par-
tu poeticon.

Sutrinas a fuendo. Varro in Hercule focratico: Qui futrinas
facere ifcius: nihil homo agis.

Scabre. Varro ī manio: Derelinquere q̃ perire fic uale fcabre
atq; alluuie & uaftitudine.

Strigofus apud ueteres morbus dicitur iumétorū: qui corpo-
ra ftrigant aut fame aut alia uitii caufa: quafi ftringofus.
Mafurius fcabrius libro. xvii. Cenfores inquit Publius Sci-
pio Nafica & Marcus Pompilius: cum equitum cenfum
agerēt: nimis ftrigofum equum & male habitum: fed equi
tem eius uberrimum & humiliffimum uiderunt.

Sufpiciofū qui ī fufpicione fit. Cato de re floriana: Sed fiqui

Modern 'Venetians' are little used today ; here are shown four designed for today's printing techniques. *Eusebius* (1924, E. F. Detterer) is an adaptation of Jenson's roman letter of 1470, and has an italic influenced by sixteenth-century chancery italic calligraphy. *Centaur* was adapted by Bruce Rogers in 1929 from his private press type of 1915, and is derived from the same Jenson original. It is much lighter in weight than true Venetians, though it exhibits all their other characteristics. The italic, originally known as Arrighi, was based on Ludovico degli Arrighi's chancery face of 1524 (Frederick Warde 1929). Stephenson Blake *Verona* originated in the la Clede Foundry, USA, where it was known as la Clede Old Style, and was bought from them on the advice of R. B. Fishenden (editor of *The Penrose Annual*, 1934–1957) about 1925.

Italian Old Style (1911) is from unknown originals ; the 12–36pt sizes were previously known as Veronese (series 59), and were transferred to this series in 1967.

RQENbaegn
baegn

Enlarged from
30pt Ludlow Eusebius

RQENbaegn
baegn

Enlarged from
30pt Monotype 252 Centaur

RQENbaegn
baegn

Enlarged from
30pt Stephenson Blake Verona

RQENbaegn
baegn

Enlarged from
30pt Monotype 108 Italian Old Style

ABCDEFGHIJKLMNOPQRSTUVWXYZ
abcdefghijklmnopqrstuvwxyzæœff fifl ffiffl
&ÆŒ£1234567890.,:;-!?"()
ABCDEFGHIJKLMNOPQRSTUVWXYZ
abcdefghijklmnopqrstuvwxyzæœfffififlffiffl
&ÆŒ£1234567890.,:;-!?"()

30pt Ludlow Eusebius

ABCDEFGHIJKLMNOPQRSTUVWXYZ
abcdefghijklmnopqrstuvwxyzæœfiflffffiffl
&ÆŒ£1234567890.,:;-!?"()
ABCDEFGHIJKLMNOPQRSTUVWXYZ
abcdefghijklmnopqrstuvwxyzæœfiflffffiffl
&ÆŒ£1234567890.,:;-!?"()

30pt Monotype 252 Centaur

ABCDEFGHIJKLMNOPQRSTUVWXYZ
abcdefghijklmnopqrstuvwxyzctst
&£1234567890.,:;-!?"
ABCDEFGHIJKLMNOPQRSTUVWXYZ
abcdefghijklmnopqrstuvwxyzæœ
&ÆŒ£1234567890.,:;-!?"()

30pt Stephenson Blake Verona

ABCDEFGHIJKLMNOPQRSTUVWXYZ
abcdefghijklmnopqrstuvwxyzæœfiflffffffiffl
&ÆŒ£1234567890.,:;-!?"()
ABCDEFGHIJKLMNOPQRSTUVWXYZ
abcdefghijklmnopqrstuvwxyzæœfiflffffffiffl
&ÆŒ£1234567890.,:;-!?"()

30pt Monotype 108 Italian Old Style

The roman type of Nicholas Jenson has been very highly praised by expert typographers during the last seventy years. But fourteen years after Jenson's death a new roman appeared, also in Venice, which attracted little notice after the sixteenth century until quite recently, in the nineteen-twenties, when Stanley Morison supervised the revival and recutting of historic types at the Monotype Corporation. In 1495 the great Renaissance publisher Aldus Manutius brought out a book with a new design of capitals. Though roughly cut, they blended a good deal better with the lower case than the obtrusive capitals of Jenson's roman. Later the same year Aldus published Bembo's *De Aetna,* using the same capitals but with a new lower case cut by his great punch-cutter Francesco Griffo of Bologna. This man's skill was strikingly demonstrated in the smaller size roman used for the *De Epidemia* of 1497. The type of *De Aetna* was used again in a reconsidered version in 1499 for the *Hypnerotomachia Poliphili* with a new alphabet of capitals.

By comparing the examples from these books on the next pages one can see a new type-design evolving which is quite distinct from Jenson's, though a development from it, as one can see from comparing Jenson's books with Aldus's. The Aldine roman is the archetype of all Old Face types which during the sixteenth century established their ascendancy over gothic throughout Europe. The quality of Aldine roman was due to the imagination and judgement of Francesco Griffo. Its important features are a calligraphic stress, the thick strokes and the serifs being at an oblique angle as in a pen script; generous letter-width, though not as wide as Jenson's, with open counters (the enclosed white area inside a letter); the capitals slightly shorter than the fairly long ascenders and descenders. The serifs are bracketed and the type shows less wear at the end of a run (Griffo may have had a harder type metal than Jenson); the crossbar of the e is rather high and horizontal. The counter of the e is therefore small, as is the bowl of the a. The letters fit closely and evenly together and are slightly condensed, without seeming at all pinched or mean. Typefaces of this kind make up well into comfortably legible pages of solid text.

Constaninus Lascaris : Erotemata. Aldus Manutius, Venice, 1495. British Museum, London.

From De Aetna: Aldus Manutius, Venice 1495

From De Epidemia: Aldus Manutius, Venice 1497

From Hypnerotomachia Poliphili: Aldus Manutius, Venice 1499

Apart from the design of the individual letters the Aldine typography is remarkable for its plain ordinary readability; and Aldus as an accurate scholar and highly successful publisher became valued and imitated internationally. It was this success which made his stylistic innovations so influential.

The two books on this page are unremarkable among the exquisite examples of the printers' art shown elsewhere, but their modest format and low cost put them within reach of a new public, without which the enormous expansion of the printing industry throughout Europe in the next century would have been impossible.

1. Bembo: De Aetna. Aldus Manutius, Venice, 1495. British Museum, London.
2. Leonicenus: De Epidemia. Aldus Manutius, Venice, 1497. British Museum, London.

1

2

Quia noueram mores hominum; tum etiam pertentare te prorsus uolui, q̃ recte ista sentires. Sed omittamus haec iam tandem filí; atq; ad eam partem sermonis, ex qua egressi sumus, reuertamur.
B. F. Immo uero pater nec reuertamur: quid enim amplius nobiscum platanis illis? de iis enim loquebamur.
Sed (si placet) ad Aetnam potius, de qua sermo haberi coeptus est, properemus.
B. P. · Mihi uero pérplacet; ita tamen, ut ne festines: tibi enim ego omnes has pomeridianas horas dico.
Sed quoniam me impellente nimium iam extra Aetnae terminos prouecti sumus, non cómittam, ut te interpellem saepius; nisi quid erit, quod de ea ipsa te rogem. B. F. Sanè mons ipse situ, forma, magnitudine, feritate, incendiis mirus; demum tota sui qualitate ac specie longe conspicuus, et sibi uni par est. Ab aurora mare Ionium bibit; et Ca

nam mascula est sine fructu, ita fructus diuersificatur alter. n. est magnitudine lētis, alter nó grádior faba (ut diximus) hic at.é qué Auicéna magnū uocat ad altez. æqualé lēti cóparatū. Hæc igitur si uera sunt (ut certe uera eē existimamus) nó paz illi decipiuntur, q̃ alluati q̃rtā faciūt safati spēm, qui q̃ safati nó tā cutis caput itegétis, quātū faciei morbū eē arbitrātur, quo ét errore ducti uidétur q̃ morbū gallicū safati eē opinātur, quoniā hic morbus cæteris ptibus sub ueste latétibus uultus hoīum euidétius offédit. Eiusdé uero erroris auctores aiūt ex.i. libro Galeni de dece tractatibus suos se sermóes súpsisse neq; aia duertūt, q̃ idé auctor de morbis faciei nó prio libro, sed q̃nto tātū illoz tractatuū edisserit, sic. n. rectus ordo exigebat, ut primum a caluariæ morbis ichoaret, de q̃bus solis i.i. libro ptractat, déide ad ea, q̃i auribz, i oculis, atq; i tota facie oriūtur mala descédés singula in propriis tractatibus declararet, ut uel ex iis q̃ ipsi cócedūt illd probari possit safati eē solius uerticis passioné. q̃do á Galéo i.i. lib. decé tractatuū de safati agitur. Sed & achores, & faui, & psydracia, & exanthemata, & q̃cūq; i eodé libro capitis morbi a galeno cónumerátur, uel tinea sūt, uel tineæ similes fœditates, súpto tamé tineæ uocabulo i eo, quo medici iuniores capiūt significatu. Quod nisi auicéna hæc oīa sub safati noīe isuis libris cópréderit uane uidebitur gloriatus q̃cqd suo opi fuerit supad ditū, eē icóprésibile, cū nusq̃ aliter de tinea, aut his tineæ affinibus affectibus egerit. Quāq̃ uero safati propriū capitis morbū statuerimus, nó tamé ignoramns morbum etiā certæ parti corporis peculiaré posse aliis aliquādo cóicari, qd ét inuit Auicenna igens safati plurimum in capite fieri. Nos quoq; ut medici de iis, quæ magna ex parte, nó autē raro, aut semp eueniūt hoc in loco differimus. Possumus ergo ita colligere. Cum morbus gallicus nó sit impetigo, ut etiā antea probauimus, neq; uero tinea, quoniā hic & ei cópares morbi, ut in capite fiūt, ita a capite incipi ūt, morbus autē Gallicus primū sui ortū habet ab obscœnis tā morbū gallcū differre á safati, quantū caput ab inguī

Hic notatur Bartholomæus cognomento Montagnana.

'Achores Faui psydracia exanthemata,

tanam suftinet imo in pede : cum fole
defcendit in infulam ,qua Tyrrenum
pelagus eft ;et quae Aeoliæ appellantur:
laterorfus , in feptentriones uergenti
Pelorus obiicitur , et Italiæ anguftiæ
funt : contra reliqua infula fiibiacet,tra-
ctifque ii omnes, qui cum Lilyboeo in
Africam protenduntur . Ipfa Aetna ra
dices fuas ferè in orbem deducit; nifi fi-
cubi orientem, et meridiémuerfus pro
miffo cliuo paulifper extenditur: celebs
degit ; et nullius montis dignata coniu-
gium cafte intra fuos terminos contine-
tur. circumitur non minus , q̃. c. mil.
paff. afcenditur ferè per uiginti ,qua bre
uior uia. Imi colles, ac omnis radicum
ambitus per oppida , et per uicos fre-
quens inhabitatur ; Baccho , Pallade ,
Cerere feraces terrae ; armentorum o-
mnis generis fupra, q̃ credas,feraciffimæ.
Hic amoeniffima loca circunquaq; : hic
fluuii perfonantes: hic obftrepentes riui:

---

ne,aut quaecunq̃ alia corporis pte eft exiftimandum.
     Ontra uero illos,qui dicunt morbum gallicum effe
  c prunam,uel igné perficũ,fiue facrũ nó eodé modo,
    ut cõtra cæteras opiniones poffumus argumétari,cũ
tanta fit apud arabes,& medicos iuniores de pruna,
& igne pfico,uel facro ambiguitas,quáta ferè de hoc ipfo mor
bo,de quo in præfentia difputamus. Alii.n.prunã,atq̃ carboné nó idé malũ fed diuerfa potius opinantur, cũ tamen. quod
ab Auicenna pruna dicitur,a Galeno libro.xiiii.artis curatiuæ.
& multis aliis in locis carbo latie ficuti ἄνθραξ græce nomine-
tur. Alii q̃uis ἄνθραξ idem græcis fignificet,quod carbo latinis,
differre tamé anthracé à carbone ea róne arbritrátur, quoniã an
traxfiat ex materia maligniore,& magis adufta,quà illa,ex qua
carbo generatur,nec defuere, qui ita defiperent,ut uerbo græ-
co latinam darent deriuationem anthracem ab antro dictum
exiftimantes,quoniam (ut inquiunt)intra concauitatem habet
abfconfam. Non abfq̃ omni tamen ratione quidam moti ui-
dentur,ut inter anthracem,atq̃ carbonem,fiue prunam diffe-
rentiam ftatuerent,cum uiderét inde Auicennam de Altoim
quem ipfi anthracem interpretantur uno capite agenté, poft
modũ altero capite de pruna tractantem tanquam démorbo
ab altoim,fiue anthrace diuerfo,ide Rafim in libro diuifionũ
deigne pfico primũ mox de anthrace feorfũ fcripfiffe. Ego ta
mé illos,q̃ inter carboné,fiue prunã,atq̃ anthracé faciũt differé
tiã libenter interrogarem nunquid Galenus de anthrace in eo
q̃ ipfi fub hoc uerbo intelligũt fignificatu ufq̃ã fecerit men
tionem,tantum enim morbum,ac magis,q̃ cæteros exitialé la
tuiffe Galenum,atque ideo neque in libro quartodecimo artif
curatiuæ,neque in fecundo ad Glauconem ,neque in libro de
tumoribus cõtra naturam,nufquam deniq̃ ab ipfo fuiffe nomi
natũ penè ridiculũ é fufpicari. Quod fi Galenus,& d̃ pruna,de
q̃ agit Auicéna,& de anthrace peftifero fub eodé noie Anthra
ce uidelicet libro.xiiii.artis curatiuæ tractaffe dicatur,quoniã an

De pruna
igne perfi-
co & anthra
ce. difputa-
tio.

Altoim

Francesco Colonna : Hypnerotomachia Poliphili.
Aldus Manutius, Venice, 1499.
Victoria and Albert Museum, London.
The typeface used in this book is the culmination of
Griffo's roman design, and the typography is equally
remarkable. The quality of the woodcut illustrations and
their perfect balance with the weight and colour of the
text were admired and closely imitated after Aldus's
death. The dramatic use of areas of text to make abstract
shapes on the page has the excitement of experimental
typography, but here achieves as well a delightfully
mellow assurance.

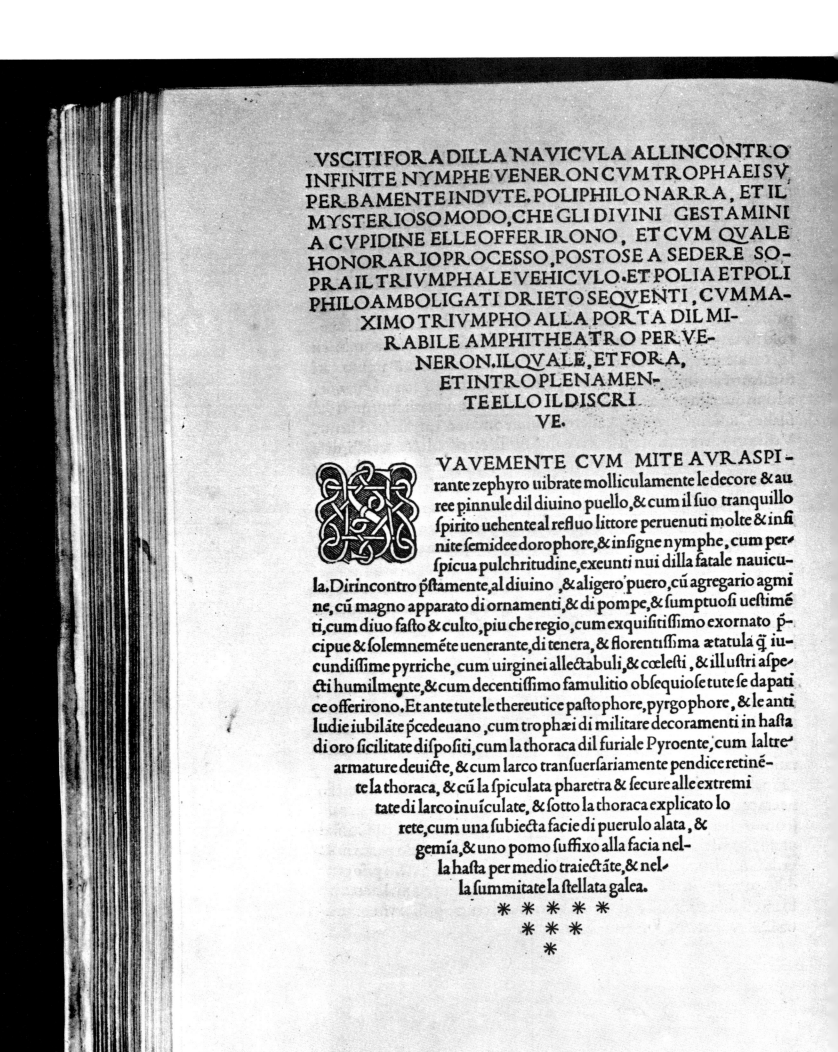

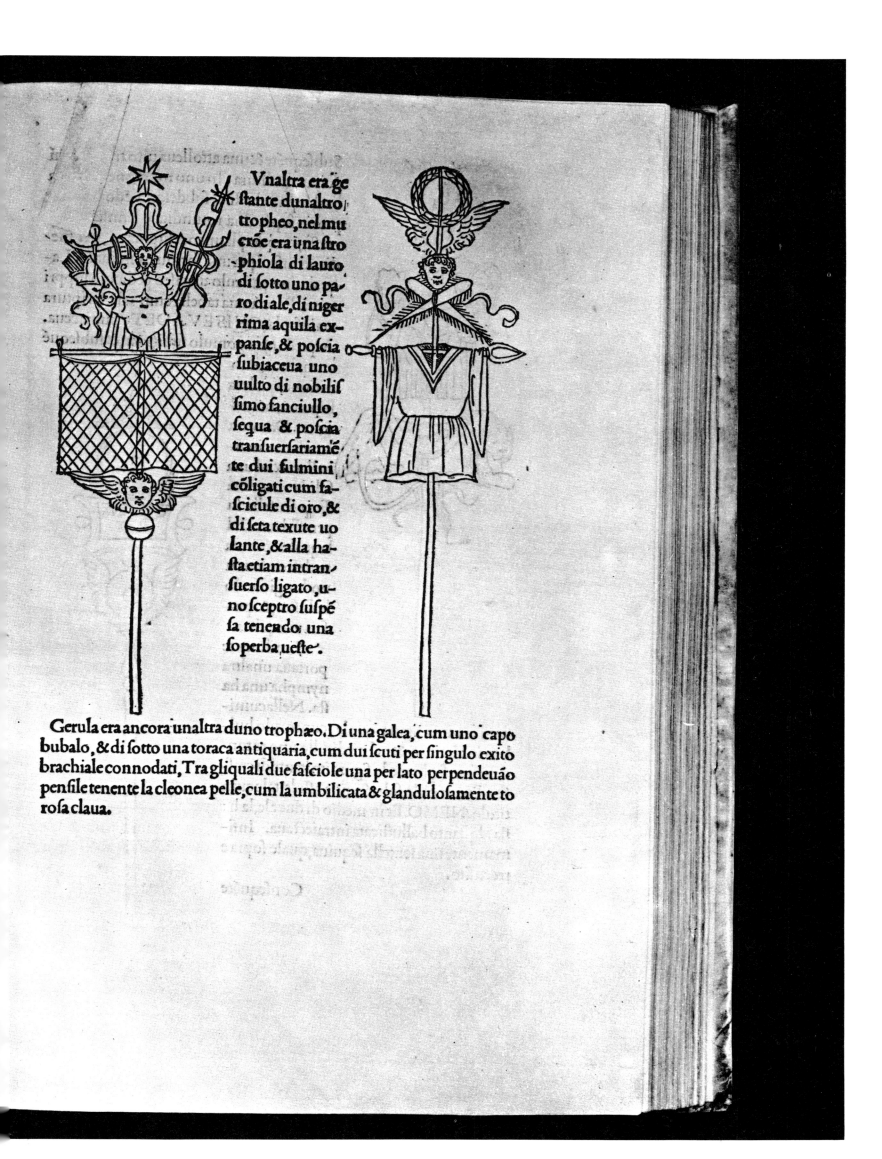

Vnaltra era ge
stante dunaltro
tropheo, nel mu
cróe era una stro
phiola di lauro
di fotto uno pa-
ro di ale, di niger
rima aquila ex-
panfe, & pofcia
fubiaceua uno
uulto di nobilif
fimo fanciullo,
fequa & pofcia
tranfuerfariamé
te dui fulmini
cóligati cum fa-
fcicule di oro, &
di feta texute uo
lante, & alla ha-
fta etiam intran
fuerfo ligato, u-
no fceptro fufpé
fa teneado una
foperba uefte.

Gerula era ancora unaltra duno trophæo. Di una galea, cum uno capo
bubalo, & di fotto una toraca antiquaria, cum dui fcuti per fingulo exito
brachiale connodati, Tra gliquali due fafciole una per lato perpendeuáo
penfile tenente la cleonea pelle, cum la umbilicata & glandulofamente to
rofa claua.

A further achievement of Aldus was the invention of italic. Pocket classics with their whole text printed in compressed, sloping lower case and upright capitals appeared soon after 1500.

They were an immediate success, chiefly because of their scholarly accuracy, and their low cost; the latter was partly due to economies in paper which the new type form made possible. But the Aldine italic (several versions of which were cut by Francesco Griffo) for all its technical mastery has not been followed by later designers. It is rather cramped and hard to read. A whole book in it must have been almost painful. Few books were printed with italic texts after 1550. Modern italics are carefully designed for use as an auxiliary alphabet, closely associated with their romans. They are mainly based on type derived from the scribes such as Arrighi and Tagliente, or upon the italics cut by Robert Granjon in the late sixteenth century.

A widespread revival of interest in this beautiful cursive script of the Renaissance, as used at the Papal Chancery, has taken place in the last thirty years: its leader is Alfred Fairbank. The first modern revival of chancery italic as a type face in its own right was by Edward Johnston in 1913.

From Virgil: Opera. Aldus Manutius, Venice 1501

1

1. Virgil: Opera. Aldus Manutius, Venice, 1501.
British Museum, London.
2. Vida: de Arte Poetica. Arrighi, Rome, 1527.
British Museum, London.

From Vida:de Arte Poetica . Arrighi, Rome 1527

.LIB. II 31

A udierant Medycumque genus, ſtirpemque Deorûm.
I am tum ille egregias curas accinxerat ardens
P ro patriæ decore, pro libertate ſepulta
A ntiquæ Auſoniæ germano fretus Iulo,
Q ui cum partitus curarum ingentia ſemper
P ondera commiſſas rerum tractabat habenas
I dem regnatorque hominum, diuumque ſacerdos .
I amque illum Europæ reges, gensque omnis in unum
C onuerſique oculos, conuerſique ora tenebant .
I amque duces animis illum concordibus omnes
V elle ſequi trepidos in Turcas arma parantem .
I llum quadriiugo inuectum per mœnia curru
R oma triumphato uidiſſes protinus orbe .
I llum Thybri pater lætanti ſpumeus alueo
E xciperes Tuſcus Tuſcum, ueheresque per undas
M iratus habitusque nouos, hominumque figuras .
I ſſent poſt currus capti longo ordine reges,
O blitusque minas minor iret barbarus hoſtis,
Q ui uictis Solymis nunc, atque oriente ſubacto
- E xultat fidens, orbisque affectat habenas

2

Although there are many Old Face designs in use today, only a few versions of Aldus's types have been developed ; but one, *Bembo*, makes up for this by its popularity as an extremely fine book face. Designed in 1929, it is derived from Aldus's *De Aetna* roman of 1495. The capitals have been lightened and regularized, and all letters, unlike Poliphilus, have been redesigned for modern use. The italic is from revised chancery types used and probably designed by Giovantonio Tagliente. *Poliphilus* was brought out before Bembo, in 1923, and is from Aldus's roman of 1499. A facsimile revival, and quite a technical achievement, it retains all the original irregularities. Unfortunately it was not copied from the best possible pages of the original, but from ones which showed the type heavier and worn ; but it possesses none the less a very useful character for some classes of work. The italic is based on letters used by Antonio Blado, 1515–67, printer to the Holy See, and designed by Arrighi in 1526. *Goudy Old Style* (1915–16), designed by F. W. Goudy for American Type Founders, was adapted by Monotype in 1929. The capitals are based on Renaissance lettering, with an Aldine letter used as a basis for the italic.

Enlarged from
30pt Monotype 270 Bembo

Enlarged from
16pt Monotype 170 Poliphilus and 119 Blado Italic

Enlarged from
30pt Monotype 291 Goudy Old Style

ABCDEFGHIJKLMNOPQRSTUVWXYZ
abcdefghijklmnopqrstuvwxyzæœffffifffiffl
&ÆŒ£1234567890.,;:-!?''()
ABCDEFGHIJKLMNOPQRSTUVWXYZ
abcdefghijklmnopqrstuvwxyzæœffffiflffiffl
&ÆŒ£1234567890.,;:-!?''()

30pt Monotype 270 Bembo

ABCDEFGHIJKLMNOPQRSTUVWXYZ
abcdefghijklmnopqrstuvwxyzæœfffiflfiffifffl
&ÆŒ£1234567890.,:;-!?''()
ABCDEFGHIJKLMNOPQRSTUVWXYZ
abcdefghijklmnopqrstuvwxyzæœffflfiffiffl
&ÆŒ£1234567890.,:;-!?''()

16pt Monotype 170 Poliphilus and 119 Blado Italic

ABCDEFGHIJKLMNOPQRSTUVWXYZ
abcdefghijklmnopqrstuvwxyzæœfiflffffffiffl
&ÆŒ£1234567890.,:;-!?''()
ABCDEFGHIJKLMNOPQRSTUVWXYZ
abcdefghijklmnopqrstuvwxyzæœfiflffffffiffl
&ÆŒ£1234567890.,:;-!?''()

30pt Monotype 291 Goudy Old Style

RQEN

baegn

baegn

Garamond's roman from Hypnerotomachia Poliphili: Jacques Kerver, Paris 1546

During the second quarter of the sixteenth century the leadership in typographic design moved to France. Books produced by the Estiennes, Geoffrey Tory, Simon de Colines, Jean de Tournes, Jacques Kerver and others were of such magnificence and distinction that their epoch became known as the Golden Age of French typography. The page became lighter and more brilliant and the illustrations and borders of printer's flowers had a new delicacy and sophistication.

The new roman type established during these years was primarily the work of the great type-cutter and founder Claude Garamond. In his early years he based his designs on Griffo's roman and Arrighi's italic. About 1530 he set up as an independent type-founder and during the 1540's cut several roman founts of type which set a style for European printers for a century. The letter was still Aldine but with a new grace and civilized assurance. The 'fit' of each letter with another, and the balance of capitals, lower case and italic provided the printer with his first comprehensive and harmonious fount of type. Modern versions of Garamond mainly follow the designs of Jannon who worked in Garamond's manner nearly a century later, but modern italics for Garamond faces are based on the type of Robert Granjon, of Lyons, whose roman and italic, together with those of Garamond himself, supplied European printers and were imported into the Netherlands by the end of the sixteenth century.

Froissart : Chroniques. de Tournes, Lyons, 1559.
Victoria and Albert Museum, London.
Garamond roman type in use.
The large size used in this chapter heading shows clearly
the masterly forms of the letters themselves and their
perfect fit and subtle harmonious rhythm, only marred by
rather too much space between the V and O in the first
line and a broken 'I' in the fourth. Modern type, particularly
for composing machines, in spite of apparent technical
mastery, cannot approach this standard of quality.

Cy commençe le tiers Volume des Croniques meſſire Iehan Froiſſart : au premier chapitre duquel il dit comment & pourquoy il ſe retira vers le Comte de Foix.   Chapitre premier.

IE me ſuis *longuement tenu à parler des beſoſignes des loïngtaines marches : mais les prochaines, quant à preſent, mont eſté ſi freſches, ſi nouuelles, & ſi enclines à ma plaiſance, que pour ce les ſay miſes arriere. Mais pourtant ne ſeiournoyent pas les vaillans hommes (qui ſe deſiroyent à auancer) ou Royaume de Caſtille & de Portugal, & auſsi bien en Gaſcongne, en Rouergue, en Quercy, en Limoſin, & en Bigorre : mais viſoyent & ſubtilloyent tous les iours, les vns ſur les autres, comme ils ſe peuſſent trouuer en party de fait-darmes, pour prendre & embler villes, chaſteaux, & fortreſſes. Et pource ie Sire Iehan Froiſſart (qui me ſuis entremis de dicter & croniquer ceſte Hiſtoire, à la requeſte, contemplation, & plaiſance, de haut Prince & renommé, meſſire Guy de Chaſtillon, Comte de Blois, Seigneur d'Aueſnes, de Beauuois, d'Eſtônehonne, & de la Geude, mon bon & ſouuerain maiſtre & Seigneur) conſideray en moy-meſme que pas n'eſtoit taillé, en long temps, que grans faits-darmes auinſſent es marches de Picardie & du païs de Flandres (puis que paix y auoit) & grandement m'ennuyoit eſtre oiſeux. car bien ſay qu'ou temps auenir (quand ie ſeray mort & pourry) ceſte noble & haute Hiſtoire ſera en grand cours : & y prendront tous Nobles & vaillans gens plaiſance, & augmentation de bien. Encores conſideray ie que i'auoye, Dieu mercy, ſens & memoire, & bonne ſouuenance de toutes les choſes paſſees, & engin cler & agu, pour conceuoir tous les faits, dont ie pourroye eſtre informé, touchans à ma principale matiere, & aage, corps, & membres, pour ſouffrir peine. Si m'auiſay que ie ne vouloye pas ſeiourner de non pourſuir ma matiere : & , pour ſauoir la verité des loingtaines beſongnes, ſans que i'y enuoyaſſe autre perſonne, en lieu de moy, pry voye raiſonnable, & †achoiſon d'aller deuers haut Prince & redouté, Maiſtre Gaſton, Comte de Foix & de Bearn : & bien ſauoye, que, ſe ie pouuoye auoir la grâce de venir en ſon hoſtel, & là eſtre à loiſir, ie ne pourroye mieux ou monde écheoir, pour eſtre informé iuſtement de toutes nouuelles (car là ſont, & ſe trouuent moult voulontiers, tous Cheualiers & Eſcuyers eſtrangers, pour la haute nobleſſe de luy) & de tout, ainſi comme ie l'imaginay, il m'en auint. Si remonſtray ce, & le voyage que ie vouloye faire, à mon treſredouté Seigneur le Comte de Blois : lequel me bailla ſes lettres de familiarité , adtéçans au Comte de Foix : & tant cheuauchay , enquerant de tous coſtés nouuelles, que par la grâce de Dieu, ſans peril & ſans dommage, ie vin en ſon hoſtel, à Ortais, ou païs de Bearn, le iour Sainéte Catherine, †l'an de grâce mil trois cens quatre vingts & huit. Lequel Comte de Foix (ſi toſt comme il me veit) me fit bonne chere : & me dit en riant, en bon François, que bien il me congnoiſſoit : & ſi ne m'auoit oncqueſmais veu : mais pluſieurs fois auoit ouy parler de moy. Si me retint

          a   en

*Annotat. 1.

†C'eſtaſſ. celles des loingtaines marches.

A la requeſte d' qui meſſire ie'han Froiſſart a compoſé le pre ſent Volume : cy voyez, en l' An notat. premiere comme les noms d'aucunes des Signeuries ſuyuantes ſont differens.

†C'eſtadire occaſion.

†En quel iour cy an arriua Froiſſart vers le Comte de Foix:

Francesco Colonna, Hypnerotomachia Poliphili;
Jacques Kerver, Paris 1546. Victoria & Albert Museum,
London.
This splendid example demonstrates the assured use of
type to make a beautiful page with the minimum use
of decoration. The initial does not interrupt the subtle
texture of the page and the whole effect is one of elegance
and distinction. It is also perfectly legible and restful to
the eye. Note the close fit of the letters which allows very
narrow word spacing.

LIVRE PREMIER DE
Comme Polia encores incongneue a Poliphi-
LE LVY MONSTRE LES IEVNES HOM-
*mes & les pucelles qui aymerent au temps iadis, & en pareil furent ay-
mees des dieux: puis luy feit veoir les Poëtes chantans leurs
poëfies immorteles.*

Peine pourroit on trouuer eloquence tant prom-
pte & si faconde qui feuft suffifante a specifier di-
ftinctement tous ces diuins fecretz & myfteres,
donner a entendre par quele prouidence ilz font
conduictz, ny pareillement exprimer la gloire, felicité, & beatitude affluente en ces quatre triumphes, accompagnez de beaux ieunes hommes, &
Nymphes gracieufes, plus cautes & prudentes en
toutes chofes, que leur ieune aage ne portoit. Ces
belles paffoient le temps ioyeufement auec leurs
amys eftans en la fleur de leur premiere ieuneffe: telement que les aucuns eftoiét
encores fans barbe, les autres ne monftroient que le petit poil follet reffemblant
a cotton delié. Plufieurs des Nymphes auoient leurs flambeaux allumez, qu'il
faifoit merueilleufement bon veoir. Il y en auoit vn grád nombre de veftues de
chappes, chafubles, & ornemens de religion. Quelques autres portoient des
lances ou pendoient certains trophees ou defpouilles antiques: & cheminoient
pefle mefle en troupe, ainfi que chacun fe trouuoit. Le bruyt, le cry, les voix
des perfonnages, & le fon des inftrumens, haultzbois, cors, trompes, buccines,
& chalemies, eftoient fi grans, qu'il fembloit que l'air fe deuft fendre. En ce lieu
de felicité viuoient les bienheureux en tout foulas & plaifir, glorifians les dieux,
& fuyuant les triumphes, parmy les beaux champs diaprez de verdure, & de
fleurs de toutes les coleurs, odeurs, & faueurs qu'il eft poffible imaginer, plus
aromatifantes que toutes les fortes d'efpices que nature fauroit produire, voire
(certes) plus belles que nulle peincture: & fans iamais eftre feichees du Soleil: car
toufiours y eft le printemps fans varier, le iour fans anuyter, & la faifon tran-
quille & temperee. Aufsi tout y croift fans labeur, & fy engendre par la bonté
de la terre, au moien de la benignité de l'air: & demeurent les fruictz, les herbes,
& les fleurs, inceffamment en leur perfection de bonté, beaulté, fenteur, & verdure, fans fleftrir ny fecher en aucune maniere. Iamais n'y a douleur ny mala-
die, deuil, foucy, melancholie, fafcherie ny defplaifir. C'eft l'habitatió de perfe-
cte beatitude, deputee pour ceux qui feruent les dieux a leur contentement. Lá
eftoit la belle Calyfto d'Arcadie, fille de Lycaon. Antiope fille de Nycteus, femme de Lycus, & mere d'Amphion le muficien. Afterie fille de Ceus le Titan,
Alcumena auec fes deux mariz, l'vn vray, & l'autre fuppofé. Puis la belle Eri-
goné, qui auoit fon gyron plein de raifins. Hellé y eftoit encores montee fur le
mouton a la toyfon d'or. Lon y pouuoit veoir Eurydice que le ferpent mordoit
au tallon. Phylira fille du vieil Ocean, & femme de Chiron le Centaure, y te-
noit

noit vn reng honnorable . Apres marçhoit la deeſſe Ceres coronnee deſpiz de
bled, montee ſur le ſerpent de Triptolemus . La belle Nymphe Lara y eſtoit ac-
compagnee de Mercure ſur la riue du Tibre tant renommé. auſsi eſtoit Iuturne
ſeur du preux Turnus : & preſque vne infinité d'autres, qui ſeroient trop lon-
gues a racompter. I'eſtoie grandement eſtonné voiant tant de gens aſſemblez
a l'entour de ces ſainctz triumphes, & ne ſauoie qu'ilz pouoient eſtre, pour ne
les auoir iamais veuz. Adonc ma guyde apperceuant mon imbecillité, ſans luy
demander que c'eſtoit, me va dire: Voy tu celle deeſſe? (en la monſtrant de bonne grace) elle a autresfois eſté mortele, mais ſa condition fut muee par auoir ay-
mé Iupiter . Ceſte autre lá fut vne tele : & telz dieux furent rauiz de ſon amour.
& ainſi pourſuyuant le catalogue, elle me declaroit leurs noms, leurs races, &
origines antiques . Apres me monſtra vne grande aſſemblee de pucelles, con-
duictes par trois matrones, marchans deuant toute la compagnie : & me dit
aucunement troublee, & changee en viſage . Mon Poliphile, ie veuil bien que
tu ſaches que nulle de celles qui ſont nees en la terre, ne peut entrer ceans ſans
auoir ſon brandon allumé par ardant amour, & violent trauail, comme tu le
me vois porter . Encores fault il que ce ſoit par le moien & addreſſe de ces trois
matrones . Puis dit en ſouſpirant: Il me conuiendra pour ton amour offrir &
eſteindre le mien dedans le ſainct temple. Ceſte parolle me penetra le cueur: tát
le plaiſir eut de force, quand ie m'ouy appeller ſien, car par ce mot elle me don-
na ſouſpeçon que c'eſtoit ma deſiree Polia: & (a la verité) tel fut mó aiſe, que l'a-
me qui me fait mouuoir, fut ſur le poinct d'abandonner mon corps, & ſe reti-
rer dans le ſien : dequoy la coleur de mon viſage m'accuſa, ioincte auec vn ſou-
ſpir bas & ardant que i'en iectay bon gré maugré: mais quãd elle ſ'en apperceut,
promptement changea de propos, me diſant: O combien il en eſt au monde
qui vouldroient ſeulement entreuoir ce qui t'eſt permis contempler a pleine
veuë! Pourtant elieue ton eſprit, & regarde ces autres damoyſelles qui vont
pair a pair auec leurs amys, chantant en beaux vers les felicitez de leurs triumphes . Ces premieres ſont les neuf Muſes , & Apollo , qui va deuant, ſuiuy
d'vne belle damoyſelle Napolitaine appellee Leria, coronnee de Laurier ver-
doiant. Aupres d'elle eſt vne fille belle par excellence, nommee Melanthie.
l'habillement, & le langage, me feirent cognoiſtre qu'elle eſtoit Greque. Ceſte la portoit vne lampe ardante, qui eſclairoit a toutes celles qui la ſuiuoient.
Son chant & ſa voix eſtoient trop plus amoureux que d'aucune autre de la
troupe. Apres ma guide me monſtra Pierus , & ſes filles, qui tant furent ſa-
uantes . Puis Lycoris, auec vne dame qui chantoit la guerre d'entre deux fre-
res de Thebes . Toutes auoient inſtrumentz de muſique, dont elles faiſoient
merueilles de ſonner. Au ſecond triumphe eſtoient la noble Corinna, Delia,
& Neera, auec pluſieurs autres Muſiciennes amoureuſes: & parmy elles Cro-
cale la Sicilienne . Au tiers triumphe ie vey Quintilia, Cynthia, & autres pro-
ferantes vers aſſez melodieux. Et là ſe trouuoit Lesbia plorant encores ſon Paſ-
ſereau. Au quatrieme precedoient Lyde, Chloe, Tiburte, et Pyrrha . Puis entre les Mainades eſtoit vne gente damoyſelle chantant pour ſon amy Phaon.
Et au derriere deux dames, l'vne bien paree de blanc, & l'autre veſtue de verd:
toutes leſquelles ſolenniſoient celle feſte, chantans a l'entour des Triumphes,

L iiij

Garamond designs, or designs by his followers, have been the source of a prolific family of modern versions. The Monotype *Garamond* of 1922 was the first type revived by the Corporation under Morison, and was based, like many other versions, on punches from the Imprimerie Royale, then attributed to Garamond but now known to be cut by Jannon about 1620. These forms, developed from Garamond's, were lighter and more open. The italic is from a fount of Granjon, about the middle of the sixteenth century. The ATF version (1917, M. F. Benton and T. M. Cleland) is also from the Jannon types. Ludlow *Garamond* (1930, R. H. Middleton) was derived from these and the Berner specimen of 1592, the italic also following Granjon. The Deberny & Peignot one, however (1912–28, George and Charles Peignot), more closely resembles the original Garamond of 1532, and has not been copied by any other founder. *Garaldus*, a name derived from Garamond and Aldus, was designed in 1957 by Aldo Novarese. The roman was developed from originals of Garamond, with very few adjustments ; its italic is a derivation from an Aldine design. *Granjon* (1928–31, supervised by G. W. Jones) is based on a sixteenth-century Paris book perhaps printed by Garamond, and despite its name has been called the best reproduction of a Garamond type today. *Estienne* (1930, G. W. Jones) is lighter than Granjon and with longer ascenders and descenders. Note the long tapering tail of the R and the large bowl of the g. The italic has a slight slope.

Enlarged from
30pt Monotype 156 Garamond

Enlarged from
30pt ATF Garamond

Enlarged from
30pt Ludlow Garamond

Enlarged from
24D Deberny & Peignot Garamond and 20D Italic

RQENbaegn

baegn

Enlarged from
28D Nebiolo Garaldus

RQENbaegn

baegn

Enlarged from
30pt Linotype (London) Granjon and 14pt Italic

RQENbaegn

baegn

Enlarged from
12pt Linotype (London) Estienne

ABCDEFGHIJKLMNOPQRSTUVWXYZ
abcdefghijklmnopqrstuvwxyz
&£1234567890.,;:-!?''()

30pt Linotype (London) Granjon and 14pt Italic

ABCDEFGHIJKLMNOPQRSTUVWXYZ
abcdefghijklmnopqrstuvwxyzæœfiflffffiffl
&ÆŒ£1234567890.,;:-!?''()

ABCDEFGHIJKLMNOPQRSTUVWXYZ
abcdefghijklmnopqrstuvwxyzæœfiflffffiffl
&ÆŒ£1234567890.,;:-!?''()

12pt Linotype (London) Estienne

ABCDEFGHIJKLMNOPQRSTUVWXYZ
abcdefghijklmnopqrstuvwxyzæœfiflffffiffl
&ÆŒ£1234567890.,;:-!?''()

ABCDEFGHIJKLMNOPQRSTUVWXYZ
abcdefghijklmnopqrstuvwxyzæœfffifflffiffl
&ÆŒ£1234567890.,;:-!?"'()
ABCDEFGHIJKLMNOPQRSTUVWXYZ
abcdefghijklmnopqrstuvwxyzæœfffifflffiffl
&ÆŒ£1234567890.,;:-!?"'()

30pt Monotype 156 Garamond

ABCDEFGHIJKLMNOPQRSTUVWXYZ
abcdefghijklmnopqrstuvwxyzfifffflffiffl&tst
&$1234567890.,-:;!?"
ABCDEFGHIJKLMNOPQRSTUVWXYZ
abcdefghijklmnopqrstuvwxyzfifffflffiffl&tst
&$1234567890.,-:;!?"

30pt ATF Garamond

ABCDEFGHIJKLMNOPQRSTUVWXYZ
abcdefghijklmnopqrstuvwxyzæœff fiflffiffl
&ÆŒ£1234567890.,:;-!?"()
ABCDEFGHIJKLMNOPQRSTUVWXYZ
abcdefghijklmnopqrstuvwxyzæœfffiflffiffl
&ÆŒ£1234567890.,:;-!?"()

30pt Ludlow Garamond

ABCDEFGHIJKLMNOPQRSTUVWXYZ
abcdefghijklmnopqrstuvwxyzæœfffiflffiffl
&ÆŒ£1234567890.,;:-!?()
ABCDEFGHIJKLMNOPQRSTUVWXYZ
abcdefghijklmnopqrstuvwxyzæœff fifl ffiffl
&ÆŒ£1234567890.,;:-!?()

28D Nebiolo Garaldus

The success of Garamond's types in his own day (and now) can be attributed to their technical excellence, as much as to their noble design. They were used throughout Europe, as Garamond and his follower Granjon were pioneer exporters of punches and matrices to printers who could not afford to employ their own type-cutters. During the course of the sixteenth century the Luther foundry at Frankfurt used French Old Face types, as did the great publishers of the Netherlands. The Plantin and Elzevir firms stood at the head of a new international centre of printing in the seventeenth century and a new robust workaday letter now known as Dutch Old Face replaced the earlier roman. Compared with Garamond the main differences are a greater weight, a bigger body to the lower-case letters, a sprightly italic, sometimes irregular in slope. Christopher van Dijck and Bartholomaeus and Dirk Voskens, working as free-lance punch-cutters during the middle of the seventeenth century, cut some of the finest types of this kind. The Dutch style was universally accepted by the end of the century when Dr Fell bought a large mixed collection of type-founts from Holland for the Oxford University Press.

ABCDEFGHIJKLMNOPQRSTUVWXYZ
abcdefghijklmnopqrstuvwxyzæœfffifffiflffifl
& Æ1234567890.,;:!?'()
ABCDEFGHIJKLMNOPQRSTUVWXYZ
abcdefghijklmnopqrstuvwxyzæœfffifflffifl
& Æ.,;:!?'()

One of the types of the Oxford University Press known as Fell Roman : the Double Pica roman and italic. It was cut at Oxford in 1682 by Peter de Walpergen.

From Salmasius : Pliny. J van de Water, Utrecht, 1689. Roman cut by Christopher van Dijck, italic from Robert Granjon's Paragon italic.

DEDICATIO.

illis plurima dixerimus, multo plura adhuc superesse dicenda ne ipse quidem livor inficiari possit. Qua de re manum de tabula tollimus *Vir Nobilissime & Gravissime*, &, ut novam hanc *Salmasii Exercitationum in Solinum Plinianarum* editionem vultu sereno & placido accipias, rogamus. Afferimus Tibi quod possumus, dum non licet quod volumus, opus non quidem nostro elaboratum ingenio, nostris tamen descriptum typis. Quod ubi Tibi non displicere intellexerimus, lætabimur, & ut divini numinis plenus Reipublicæ Ultrajectinæ rem bene geras, & serus in cœlum redeas, Deum ter Optimum Maximum supplices venerabimur.

Vir Nobilissime & Gravissime,
clientes Tibi devotissimi,

JOHANNES vande WATER.
JOHANNES RIBBIUS.
FRANCISCUS HALMA.
GUILIELMUS vande WATER.

SERE-

SERENISSIMÆ
VENETORUM
REIPUBLICÆ
CLAUDIUS SALMASIUS
S.

Um in eo essem *Sapientissimi & Illustrissimi Proceres*, ut post absolutum Exercitationum Plinianarum opus, delegendis, ut sit, patronis, & parandis ei defensoribus ex illustri aliquo loco cogitare deberem, non diu mihi dubitandum fuit, an vestrum nomen clarissimum fronti earum inscriberem, qui multo ante, ab eo nempe tempore, quo prima operis fundamenta ponere coepi, id totum vobis dicandum destinarim. Quod non solum quam libenter, sed etiam quam merito fecerim ex veteri votorum ac dedicationum formula, mea refert plurimum à me ipso praedicari, ne qui sint scilicet quibus mirum videri possit, atque etiam reprehensione dignum, me foris & apud exteros quaesivisse quod in patria ac domi possem habere, quod utique haberem. Profecto tametsi hujus mei facti nullam rationem mihi reddere liberet, non tamen ullam à me exigi magis par esset quam ab illis solet, qui vulgo aliquem sibi privata religione colendum sumunt ex adscripticiorum coelitum ordine, quem pro tutelari numine habeant, cui vota sua nuncupent, cui preces allegent, cuique adeo se in omni occasione & fortuna commendatos cupiant. Quod saepius ab his levi opinione, ac nullis, aut frivolis admodum de causis fieri videmus, quippe qui super eo interrogati nihil probabile adferant, cur hunc potius quam alium elegerint, nisi proprium quemdam affectum quo se ad hujus alicujus Divi devotionem impensius ferri fatentur. Si nihil aliud ipse sequutus essem in his monumentis laboris mei nomini vestro consecrandis, praeter hanc eamdem animi inclinationem, quam liberam unusquisque habere debet, nemini sano nomine isto reprehendendus forem. Quis enim culpare ausit in alio, quod ex aequo sibi permissum gaudeat, & indignetur vetitum? Quid autem voluntarium magis, aut minus lege alligandum, quam naturalis iste impetus, quo ad amorem & odium, qualiscunque rei vel personae impellimur? Hic ipse denique est animi motus, qui ex duobus primùm conspectis & pariter ignotis alteri nos potius favere cogit, cum alter saepe favo-

re

In so far as it throws light on the changing typography of
their books, one might suggest that Aldus supplied
Renaissance intellectuals, Garamond, French noblemen,
and the Dutch printers, the rising mercantile classes.

But the variations are changes in emphasis only, and the
line of development of Old Face types from Griffo to
Caslon is unbroken.

inet imo in pede : cum fole
n infulam , qua Tyrrenum
;et quae Aeoliæ appellantur:
in feptentriones uergenti
piicitur , et Italiae anguftiae

tres de familiarité , adréçans au
tous coftés nouuelles, que par la
fon hoftel, à Ortais, ou païs de B
cens quatre vingts & huit. Lequ
bonne chere : & me dît en riant,
m'auoit oncquefmais veu : mais

defcriptum typis. Quod ub
tellexerimus ; lætabimur ,
nus Reipublicæ Ultrajectin
rus in cœlum redeas , De
mum fupplices venerabimu

Quoufque tandem abu-
tere, Catilina, patientia
noftra ? quamdiu nos e-
tiam furor ifte tuus elu-
Quoufque tandem abutere,

William Caslon, the first English type-founder to satisfy the growing demand from English printers, followed the Dutch model in his splendid roman started in 1725.

This roman type met with immediate and enduring success not only because of its inherent merits, but because it supplied English printers with type where formerly they had to import it. Caslon met their needs so satisfactorily for most of the eighteenth century that changes in style were slow to make any impact. In spite of the typographical innovations of Baskerville and F. A. Didot, Caslon remained 'the' roman for most printers until well into the nineteenth century.

Caslon marks the end of the so-called Old Face period during which the roman alphabet of caps, lower case and italic gradually established itself as the standard means of expression for the printed word in Europe. The changes of form in these letters show how designers for more than 200 years and in different countries made the alphabet respond to their wishes, and the needs of their times.

RQEN
baegn
baegn

From a Caslon type specimen of 1734

*e beginning of idolatry, 23 and the
 . 30 God will punish them that
 by their idols.*

ne preparing himself to sail, and
 to pass through the raging
h upon a piece of wood, more
he || vessel that carrieth him.

ily desire of gain devised || that,
kman built it by his skill.

y providence, O Father, go—
for thou hast ᵃ made a way in
a safe path in the waves:

g that thou canst save from all
, though a man went to sea

heless thou wouldest not that
f thy wisdom should be idle,
e do men commit their lives
ece of wood, and passing the
a weak vessel, are saved.

n the old time also, when the
s perished, the hope of the
ned by thy hand, escaped in a
and left to all ages a seed of

ssed is the wood whereby righ-
neth.

hat which is made with hands
well it, as he that made it: he
 made it; and it, because being
it was called god.

ne ungodly and his ungodliness
e hateful unto God.

hat which is made shall be puer with him that made it.

ore even || upon the idols of
shall there be a visitation: be-
creature of God they are be-
omination, and ᵉ † stumbling-
souls of men, and a || snare to
he unwise.

e devising of idols was the be-
iritual fornication, and the in-
em the corruption of life.

17 Whom men could not honour || in presence, because they dwelt far off, they took the counterfeit of his visage, from far, and made an express image of a king whom they honoured, to the end that by this their forwardness, they might flatter him that was absent, as if he were present.

18 Also the singular diligence of the artificer did help to set forward the ignorant to more superstition.

19 For he peradventure willing to please one in authority, forced all his skill to make the resemblance, † of the best fashion.

20 And so the multitude allured by the grace of the work, took him now for a god, which a little before was but honoured as a man.

21 And this was an occasion to deceive the world: for men serving either calamity or tyranny, did ascribe unto stones and stocks, the incommunicable || name.

22 Moreover, this was not enough for them, that they erred in the knowledge of God, but whereas they lived in the great war of ignorance, those so great plagues called they peace.

23 For whilst they ᶠ slew their children in sacrifices, or used secret ceremonies, or made revellings of strange rites;

24 They kept neither lives nor marriages any longer undefiled: but either one slew another traiterously, or grieved him by adultery.

25 So that there reigned in all men || without exception, blood, man-slaughter, theft and dissimulation, corruption, unfaithfulness, tumults, perjury,

26 Disquieting of good men, forgetfulness of good turns, defiling of souls, changing of || kind, disorder in marriages, adultery, and shameless uncleanness.

27 For the worshipping of idols † not to be named, is the beginning, the cause, and the end of all evil.

† Gr. to the better.

|| of God.

ᶠ Deut. 18. 10. Jer. 7. 9. & 19. 4.

|| Or, confusedly.

|| Or, sex.

† Gr. nameless.

1. Bible, John Baskett, Oxford, 1716. This makes use of Fell Roman. Rules in red.
2. Life of Newton, printed by Samuel Palmer, 1728. Caslon Great Primer text, with heading and figures in Double Pica Fell Roman. St Bride Printing Library, London.

2

and the water as moving in it : and the water in respect of the vessel has the greatest motion, when the vessel first begins to turn, and loses this relative motion more and more, till at length it quite ceases. But now, when the vessel first begins to turn, the surface of the water remains smooth and flat, as before the vessel began to move; but as the motion of the vessel communicates by degrees motion to the water, the surface of the water will be observed to change, the water subsiding in the middle and rising at the edges: which elevation of the water is caused by the parts of it pressing from the axis, they move about; and therefore this force of receding from the axis of motion depends not upon the relative motion of the water within the vessel, but on its absolute motion ; for it is least, when that relative motion is greatest, and greatest, when that relative motion is least, or none at all.

95. THUS the true cause of what appears in the surface of this water cannot be assigned, without considering the water's motion within the vessel. So also in the system of the world, in order to find out the cause of the planetary motions, we must know more of the real motions, which belong to each planet, than is absolutely necessary for the uses of astronomy. If the astronomer should suppose the earth to stand still, he could ascribe such motions to the celestial bodies, as should answer all the appearances; though he would not account for them in so simple a manner, as by attributing motion to the earth. But the motion of the earth must of necessity be considered, before the real causes, which actuate the planetary system, can be discovered.

CHAP.

The multiplicity of types in the Dutch Old Face style has resulted in a large and varied collection of modern developments. Their mercantile background, too, may have made them more useful models for much of today's printing. One of the most widely used designs, however, *Plantin* (1913, F. H. Pierpoint), is actually from a Granjon face, used by successors of the printer Christopher Plantin, of Antwerp, working during the sixteenth century; it was also being used in Frankfurt and Basle about 1570. The modern version is the first type designed for art paper and, with its large x-height, was a pioneer attempt to make types more economical in paper. *Van Dijck* (1935, with assistance from Van Krimpen) is from a roman appearing in an Amsterdam edition of Ovid, printed in 1671, but not definitely by Van Dijck himself. Stempel *Janson* is from the original matrices, held by Stempel since 1920; while the Linotype version of 1937, by C. H. Griffiths, is based on an original of 1670–90, cut by Nicholas Kis, of Amsterdam, (according to Stempel by Janson himself); *Ehrhardt* (1938) is a regularized version of a type by Kis of 1672. Monotype *Caslon* (1915) is an accurate recutting of revived Caslon types; Linotype *Caslon* was cut in 1921.

The Haas *Caslon* uses the founder's own matrices in small sizes; larger sizes were cut in 1944.

RQENbaegn *baegn*

Enlarged from
30pt Monotype 110 Plantin

RQENbaegn *baegn*

Enlarged from
30pt Monotype 203 Van Dijck

RQENbaegn *baegn*

Enlarged from
28D Stempel Janson

RQENbaegn *baegn*

Enlarged from
12pt Linotype (London) Janson

RQENbaegn
baegn

RQENbaegn
baegn

RQENbaegn
baegn

RQENbaegn
baegn

Imprint (1912, with assistance from Edward Johnston and J. H. Mason) is derived from late eighteenth-century types, including Caslon. It was the first original book type designed especially for machine composition, and was cut for Gerard Meynell and his magazine *The Imprint*. *Old Style* (1922) is from a derivation of Miller &

Richard's Old Style of 1852, cut by Alexander Phemister; from the same source, Old Style (series 2), used for the text setting at the back of this atlas, dates from 1901.

RQENbaegn
baegn

Enlarged from
30pt Monotype 101 Imprint

RQENbaegn
baegn

Enlarged from
30pt Monotype 151 Old Style

ABCDEFGHIJKLMNOPQRSTUVWXYZ
abcdefghijklmnopqrstuvwxyzæœffffifflffifffl
&ÆŒ£1234567890.,;:-!?"'()
ABCDEFGHIJKLMNOPQRSTUVWXYZ
abcdefghijklmnopqrstuvwxyzæœfiflffffifffl
&ÆŒ£1234567890.,:;-!?"'()

30pt Monotype 110 Plantin

ABCDEFGHIJKLMNOPQRSTUVWXYZ
abcdefghijklmnopqrstuvwxyzæœfiflffffifffl
&ÆŒ£1234567890.,:;-!?"'()
ABCDEFGHIJKLMNOPQRSTUVWXYZ
abcdefghijklmnopqrstuvwxyzæœfiflffffifffl
&ÆŒ£1234567890.,:;-!?"'()

30pt Monotype 203 Van Dijck

ABCDEFGHIJKLMNOPQRSTUVWXYZ
abcdefghijklmnopqrstuvwxyzæœefffifl
&ÆŒ1234567890.,-:;!?'(),,""»«/[]§*
ABCDEFGHIJKLMNOPQRSTUVWXYZ
abcdefghijklmnopqrstuvwxyzæœfffifl
&ÆŒ1234567890.,-:;!?'(),,""»«[]§†*&

28D Stempel Janson

ABCDEFGHIJKLMNOPQRSTUVWXYZ
abcdefghijklmnopqrstuvwxyzæœfiflffffiffl
&ÆŒ £1234567890.,;:-!?"()

12pt Linotype (London) Janson

ABCDEFGHIJKLMNOPQRSTUVWXYZ
abcdefghijklmnopqrstuvwxyzæœfiflfffiffl
&ÆŒ £1234567890.,;:-!?"()

ABCDEFGHIJKLMNOPQRSTUVWXYZ
abcdefghijklmnopqrstuvwxyzæœefffififlffiffl
&ÆŒ£1234567890.,;:-!?"()
ABCDEFGHIJKLMNOPQRSTUVWXYZ
abcdefghijklmnopqrstuvwxyzæœfffiflffiffl
&ÆŒ£1234567890.,;:-!?"()

30pt Monotype 128 Caslon

ABCDEFGHIJKLMNOPQRSTUVWXYZ
abcdefghijklmnopqrstuvwxyz
&$1234567890.,;:-!?"()
ABCDEFGHIJKLMNOPQRSTUVWXYZ
abcdefghijklmnopqrstuvwxyz
&$1234567890.,;:-!?"()

30pt Linotype (Mergenthaler) Caslon and 24pt Italic

ABCDEFGHIJKLMNOPQRSTUVWXYZ
abcdefghijklmnopqrstuvwxyzæœefffiflft
&ÆŒ1234567890.,;:-!?'„()
ABCDEFGHIJKLMNOPQRSTUVWXYZ
abcdefghijklmnopqrstuvwxyzæœfiflft
&ÆŒ1234567890.,;:-!?'„()

28D Haas Caslon

ABCDEFGHIJKLMNOPQRSTUVWXYZ
abcdefghijklmnopqrstuvwxyzæœfiflffffiffl
&ÆŒ£1234567890.,:;-!?"()
ABCDEFGHIJKLMNOPQRSTUVWXYZ
abcdefghijklmnopqrstuvwxyzæœfiflffffiffl
&ÆŒ£1234567890.,:;-!?"()

24pt Monotype 453 Ehrhardt

ABCDEFGHIJKLMNOPQRSTUVWXYZ
abcdefghijklmnopqrstuvwxyzæœfiflffffiffl
&ÆŒ£1234567890.,:;-!?"()
ABCDEFGHIJKLMNOPQRSTUVWXYZ
abcdefghijklmnopqrstuvwxyzæœfiflffffiffl
&ÆŒ£1234567890.,:;-!?"()

30pt Monotype 101 Imprint

ABCDEFGHIJKLMNOPQRSTUVWXYZ
abcdefghijklmnopqrstuvwxyzæœfiflffffiffl
&ÆŒ£1234567890.,:;-!?' '()
ABCDEFGHIJKLMNOPQRSTUVWXYZ
abcdefghijklmnopqrstuvwxyzæœfiflffffiffl
&ÆŒ£1234567890.,:;-!?"()

30pt Monotype 151 Old Style

A change in emphasis of a radical kind was made in France at the end of the seventeenth century. An exclusive Royal roman was cut by Philippe Grandjean for Louis XIV which froze the Renaissance humanity in the old style roman. It was based on the Academy's model roman, a mathematically drawn alphabet. The new face had flat unbracketed serifs and a strong emphasis on the verticals. The lower case 'l' of this Romain du Roi has a curious spur on its stem ; copied from an old script flourish, it is an unmistakable mark of identity like the deliberate mistakes on a banknote.

RQEN

baegn l

baegn

From Les Médailles : Imprimerie Royale, Paris 1702

The result on the printed page was a haughty brilliance, quite appropriate to its purpose. Although exclusive to the Imprimerie Royale, the new roman was copied, and its character influenced the new designers of the eighteenth century.

Académie des inscriptions et belles lettres : Les médailles sur les principaux événements du règne de Louis-le-Grand. Imprimerie Royale, Paris, 1702.
Victoria and Albert Museum, London.

Fleischman's roman of 1734 and Fournier's of 1750 are clearly in the new style. The pretty little books of eighteenth-century France also reject the fat bourgeois typography of Dutch roman.

One of the most important documents in the history of typography, Fournier's two-volume technical manual and type specimen (shown opposite) also contains the final form of the point system developed by him. This was the basis of the European point system (later modified by Didot) currently in use. As well as a very full range of roman types, Fournier offered exotic scripts and these particularly fine decorated letters.

Manuel Typographique : P. S. Fournier, Paris 1764
St Bride Printing Library, London

Nº. LXXIV. 72

TRISMÉGISTE.

Le Soleil, ainſi que la mort, ne ſe peut point regarder fixement.

Nº. LXXV. 73

TRISMÉGISTE.

Chacun a ſa façon de s'exprimer qui vient de ſa façon de ſentir.

92 *LETTRES*

de Gros-canon.

GB
SE

Moyennes de fonte.

NI

DE DEUX POINTS. 93

Moyennes de fonte.

IG

Groſſes de fonte.

FJ

The Monotype *Fournier* of 1925 must stand as our only example of an early Transitional type in use today. It is a facsimile of one of Fournier's medium text types (St Augustin Ordinaire) in his Manuel Typographique of 1764. During the development of the Monotype version, two designs were experimentally cut; by mistake, the wrong one was chosen for production, the aborted design (series 178) being rather bolder and less spidery. It has recently been brought out in a full range of text sizes.

RQENbaegn
baegn

Enlarged from
30pt Monotype 185 Fournier and 18pt Italic

ABCDEFGHIJKLMNOPQRSTUVWXYZ
abcdefghijklmnopqrstuvwxyzæœfiflffffiffl
&ÆŒ£1234567890.,:;-!?''()

ABCDEFGHIJKLMNOPQRSTUVWXYZ
abcdefghijklmnopqrstuvwxyzæœfiflffffiffl
&ÆŒ£1234567890.,:;-!?''()

30pt Monotype 185 Fournier and 18pt Italic

RQEN

baegn

baegn

From Paradise Lost: John Baskerville, Birmingham 1765

Caslon's achievement in the 1720's was of the greatest importance to English printers during the eighteenth century. For the first time a larger range of fine roman types was available with which all kinds of work could be done without the need to import faces from European founders. But the design, as we have said, was derivative. The designer who made the first original contribution to type design in England, John Baskerville, had little commercial success in his lifetime though versions of his types are among the most popular book faces today. He was a Birmingham japanner, a letter-cutter and a writing master, and in his roman of 1754 these disciplines produced magnificently controlled, generously proportioned letterforms. It is an original design of great distinction, which echoes the architecture of the Augustan Age in its serenity and masculinity; it holds a central position in the transitional group of typefaces.

Baskerville made a number of important innovations in ink and papermaking and printing. Passing wove paper through hot copper cylinders produced a smooth white surface that showed off the black type magnificently. He also developed a new open typographic style with wide margins and leading between the lines. This gave the page an austere brilliance. Instead of illustration, the letters decorate the pages. But while Baskerville was not commercially successful in England, his work was admired and imitated here and abroad.

84 *P.VIRGILII GEORGICA* LIB. III.

Sævit et in lucem Stygiis emiſſa tenebris
Pallida Tiſiphone: morbos agit ante metumque;
Inque dies avidum ſurgens caput altius effert.
Balatu pecorum, et crebris mugitibus amnes,
555 Arenteſque ſonant ripæ, colleſque ſupini:
Jamque catervatim dat ſtragem, atque aggerat ipſis
In ſtabulis turpi dilapſa cadavera tabo:
Donec humo tegere, ac foveis abſcondere diſcunt.
Nam neque erat coriis uſus; nec viſcera quiſquam
560 Aut undis abolere poteſt, aut vincere flamma:
Nec tondere quidem morbo illuvieque pereſa
Vellera, nec telas poſſunt attingere putres.
Verum etiam, inviſos ſi quis tentarat amictus,
Ardentes papulæ, atque immundus olentia ſudor
565 Membra ſequebatur: nec longo deinde moranti
Tempore, contactos artus ſacer ignis edebat.

P. VIR-

P. VIRGILII MARONIS

GEORGICON.

LIBER QUARTUS.

Protinus aerii mellis cœleſtia dona
Exſequar. hanc etiam, Mæcenas, aſpice partem.
Admiranda tibi levium ſpeƈtacula rerum,
Magnanimoſque duces, totiuſque ordine gentis
5 Mores, et ſtudia, et populos, et prælia dicam.
In tenui labor, at tenuis non gloria: ſi quem
Numina læva ſinunt, auditque vocatus Apollo.
Principio ſedes apibus ſtatioque petenda,
Quo neque ſit ventis aditus, (nam pabula venti
10 Ferre domum prohibent) neque oves hœdique petulci
Floribus inſultant, aut errans bucula campo
Decutiat rorem, et ſurgentes atterat herbas.
Abſint et piƈti ſqualentia terga lacerti
Pinguibus a ſtabulis, meropeſque, aliæque volucres;
15 Et manibus Progne peƈtus ſignata cruentis.
Omnia nam late vaſtant, ipſaſque volantes
Ore ferunt, dulcem nidis immitibus eſcam.
At liquidi fontes, et ſtagna virentia muſco
Adſint, et tenuis fugiens per gramina rivus;
20 Palmaque veſtibulum aut ingens oleaſter obumbret:
Ut, quum prima novi ducent examina reges
Vere ſuo, ludetque favis emiſſa juventus;
Vicina invitet decedere ripa calori,

L 3   Obvia-

Baskerville's types have been as important a source for modern designs as have those of Garamond, and are the major source of mid-Transitional types. The Monotype version of 1923 is a regularized version of the 1757 Virgil Great Primer fount, and in 1931 Linotype brought out a fairly true recutting of the Deberny & Peignot version which was acually cast from matrices made from Baskerville's punches. *Fry's Baskerville* is much later in feeling than the original, and has more in common with Bell or Scotch Roman than with Baskerville. This 'improved' version was cut by Isaac Moore for Dr Fry in 1769, and reproduced by Stephenson Blake in 1913. The 30pt and larger sizes were engraved and cut by them; an italic exists, but is not supplied by the founder. *Georgian* (1925, G. W. Jones) is primarily based on a design by Alexander Wilson of about 1790, perhaps also for Dr Fry. *Fontana* (1936, under the direction of Dr Giovanni Mardersteig) was designed for William Collins Sons & Co. Ltd for their exclusive use and was closely copied from a fount of Alexander Wilson of about 1760. The height of the capitals has been slightly reduced, but it is otherwise fairly accurate. In 1961 it was made generally available.

RQENbaegn *baegn*

Enlarged from
30pt Monotype 169 Baskerville

RQENbaegn *baegn*

Enlarged from
12pt Linotype (London) Baskerville

RQENbaegn *baegn*

Enlarged from
30D Deberny & Peignot Baskerville and 24D Italic

RQENbaegn

Enlarged from
30pt Stephenson Blake Fry's Baskerville

RQENbaegn
baegn

Enlarged from
12pt Linotype (London) Georgian

RQENbaegn
baegn

Enlarged from
18pt Monotype 403 Fontana

ABCDEFGHIJKLMNOPQRSTUVWXYZ
abcdefghijklmnopqrstuvwxyzæœfffifIflffiffl
&ÆŒ£1234567890.,;:-!?''()

ABCDEFGHIJKLMNOPQRSTUVWXYZ

abcdefghijklmnopqrstuvwxyzæœfffifIflffiffl

&ÆŒ£1234567890.,;:-!?''()

30pt Monotype 169 Baskerville

ABCDEFGHIJKLMNOPQRSTUVWXYZ
abcdefghijklmnopqrstuvwxyzæœfiflffffiffl
&ÆŒ£1234567890.,;:-!?''()

ABCDEFGHIJKLMNOPQRSTUVWXYZ
abcdefghijklmnopqrstuvwxyzæœfiflffffiffl
&ÆŒ£1234567890.,;:-!?''()

12pt Linotype (London) Baskerville

ABCDEFGHIJKLMNOPQRSTUVWXYZ
abcdefghijklmnopqrstuvwxyzœflfifffffiffl
&Œ1234567890.,;:-!?"()

ABCDEFGHIJKLMNOPQRSTUVWXYZ

abcdefghijklmnopqrstuvwxyzœflfifffffiffl

Œ1234567890.,;:-!?"()

30D Deberny & Peignot Baskerville and 24D Italic

ABCDEFGHIJKLMNOPQRSTUVWXYZ
abcdefghijklmnopqrstuvwxyzfffifIflffiffl
&£1234567890.,;:-!?"

30pt Stephenson Blake Fry's Baskerville

ABCDEFGHIJKLMNOPQRSTUVWXYZ
abcdefghijklmnopqrstuvwxyzæœfiflffffiffl
&ÆŒ£1234567890.,;:-!?''()

ABCDEFGHIJKLMNOPQRSTUVWXYZ
abcdefghijklmnopqrstuvwxyzæœfiflffffiffl
&ÆŒ£1234567890.,;:-!?''()

12pt Linotype (London) Georgian

ABCDEFGHIJKLMNOPQRSTUVWXYZ
abcdefghijklmnopqrstuvwxyzæœfffIflfiffiffl
&ÆŒ£1234567890., :;-!?''()
ABCDEFGHIJKLMNOPQRSTUVWXYZ
abcdefghijklmnopqrstuvwxyzæœffflfifffiffl
&ÆŒ1234567890.,:;-!?

18pt Monotype 403 Fontana

The trends in letter design developed by Baskerville were taken a stage further by William Martin and Richard Austin at the end of the century. Fry's Baskerville, Bell and Scotch Roman are designs which accentuate the sharpness of cut in Baskerville's roman. The serifs become pointed and tapered and the letters rather condensed. Whereas Baskerville's type shows his background as a writing master and letter-cutter, his followers' work is very much the product of the engraving tool and matches the woodcuts and copper plates of the illustrators of the time.

THE TRAVELLER.

Remote, unfriended, melancholy, slow,

Or by the lazy Scheld, or wandering Po;

Or onward, where the rude Carinthian boor

Against the houseless stranger shuts the door;

Or where Campania's plain forsaken lies,

A weary waste, expanding to the skies;

Where-e'er I roam, whatever realms to see,

My heart, untravell'd, fondly turns to thee:

Still to my Brother turns, with ceaseless pain,

And drags at each remove a lengthening chain.

Goldsmith's Poems. William Bulmer, London, 1795.
Types by William Martin. Woodcuts by John Bewick.
Victoria and Albert Museum, London.

If these late Transitional types here are compared with those on pages 62–3 (and Fry's Baskerville could well be included on this page), the general trend of development can clearly be seen – unconsciously leading towards Moderns. It is interesting that now the new versions are often simply accurate recuttings of the originals. The Monotype *Bell* of 1931, for instance, is a facsimile copy from punches cut in 1788 by Richard Austin for John Bell which, together with the matrices, have descended to Stephenson Blake. *Bulmer* (1928, M. F. Benton) is from original cuttings by William Martin for William Bulmer of the Shakespeare Press about 1790 ; the new design is a little more 'modern face' than the original. The Monotype version (1936) used for the text setting at the back of this atlas was originally produced only in 11 pt and 12 pt ; but the range of sizes is now to be extended. Monotype *Scotch Roman* (1920) was cut for the printers R. & R. Clark, and is an accurate recutting of the Miller & Richard type of 1810. Series 46 (1907) is used for the text settings ; this is a revival of letters derived from the same model as Monotype Series 137.

The Linotype version, the apparent boldness of which, as shown here, is partly due to the greater enlargement compared with the Monotype version, is derived from similar sources.

Enlarged from
30pt Monotype 341 Bell

Enlarged from
30pt ATF Bulmer

Enlarged from
30pt Monotype 137 Scotch Roman

Enlarged from
10pt Linotype (London) Scotch Roman

ABCDEFGHIJKLMNOPQRSTUVWXYZ
abcdefghijklmnopqrstuvwxyzæœfiflfffffiffl
& ÆŒ£1234567890.,:;-!?''()
ABCDEFGHIJKLMNOPQRSTUVWXYZ
abcdefghijklmnopqrstuvwxyzæœfiflfffffiffl
&ÆŒ£1234567890.,:;-!?''()

30pt Monotype 341 Bell

ABCDEFGHIJKLMNOPQRSTUVWXYZ
abcdefghijklmnopqrstuvwxyzfifffflffiffl
&$1234567890.,-:;!?''
ABCDEGFHIJKLMNOPQRSTUVWXYZ
abcdefghijklmnopqrstuvwxyzfifffflfflffi
&$1234567890.,-:;!?''

30pt ATF Bulmer

ABCDEFGHIJKLMNOPQRSTUVWXYZ
abcdefghijklmnopqrstuvwxyzæœfiflfffffiffl
&ÆŒ£1234567890.,:;-!?''()
ABCDEFGHIJKLMNOPQRSTUVWXYZ
abcdefghijklmnopqrstuvwxyzæœfiflfffffiffl
&ÆŒ£1234567890.,:;-!?''()

30pt Monotype 137 Scotch Roman

ABCDEFGHIJKLMNOPQRSTUVWXYZ
abcdefghijklmnopqrstuvwxyzæœfiflfffffiffl
&ÆŒ£1234567890.,:;-!?''()
10pt Linotype (London) Scotch Roman

ABCDEFGHIJKLMNOPQRSTUVWXYZ
abcdefghijklmnopqrstuvwxyzæœfiflfffiffl
&ÆŒ£1234567890.,:;-!?''()

RQEN

baegn

baegn

From Manuale Tipografico : Bodoni, Parma 1818

European admiration for Baskerville's typography resulted in a design at the turn of the century which heralded a new age.

The Modern romans of Didot, Bodoni and, later, Walbaum (in the manner of copperplate) concentrated on brilliant contrast and striking effect. They were types designed to impress the eye, not for comfortable legibility. The fine hairlines and the abrupt and exaggerated changes from thick to thin demanded a sophisticated printing technique and smoother paper of the highest quality ; given these the new style was certainly astonishing.

The letters themselves are beautifully designed shapes, drawn with sophisticated and rather aristocratic taste.

They were, however, the expression of the French revolution as much as of fine neo-classical printing, and the Napoleonic Empire. But drawn letters which have no reference to written forms tend to lack the subtle rhythms of a good text face.

The brilliance and novelty of the new design led to its wide use for general printing throughout the nineteenth century, but its inherent weaknesses and the poor standards of design of the printing industry resulted in a miserable grey mediocrity, which we discuss on a later page.

Opposite : Dedication from Oratio Dominica : Bodoni, Parma, 1806.

A

EVGENIO · NAPOLEONE

PER · LODE

CHE · TVTTE · L'ALTRE · IN · SÉ · ADVNA

DI

NAPOLEONE · IL · GRANDE

IMPERATOR · DE' FRANCESI

RE · D'ITALIA

FIGLIO · ADOTTIVO

VICE-RE · D'ITALIA

ARCI-CANCELLIERE · DI · STATO

DELL' IMPERO · FRANCESE

PRINCIPE · DI · VENEZIA ECC. ECC.

E

AD · AVGVSTA · AMALIA

FIGLIA

DI · MASSIMILIANO · RE · DI · BAVIERA

CONSORTE · DI · LUI · IMPAREGGIABILE

AMABILISSIMA

Dante : Divina Comedia. Bodoni, Parma, 1796.
St Bride Printing Library, London.
Strict discipline, simplicity and assurance married to
fastidious presswork, together with the brilliant new
roman and italic, make this typical Bodoni page sparkle
like fallen snow.

Vieni dunque, o SIGNOR *, vieni, e l'affetto*
E il desiderio universal consola;
E a raddoppiar la nostra gioja teco
Venga, degna di te, l'augusta Sposa,
Nuovo ornamento a questi lidi, e nuovo
Felice innesto, onde la chiara in terra,
E protetta dal ciel, Borbonia pianta
Più bella ognor su questo suol verdeggi,
E nuovi rami germogliando stenda
Le amiche braccia, e in sue radici eterna
Di placid'ombra e preziosi frutti
Protegga e nutra le Parmensi rive.

A' STUDIOSI

DEL DIVINO POETA

GIO: JACOPO MARCH. DIONISI

CANONICO DI VERONA.

I

Dalla letterata Firenze, dall'intimo seno
delle sue Biblioteche ho tratta, Signori, con
un po' di destrezza e un po' più di pazienza
nell'anno 1789 la divina Commedia di stra-
niere brutture purgata, e di natíe bellezze
riadorna, la quale or esce felicemente alla
luce. Io la serbava, come cosa cara, per me,
avendo fisso nell'animo di pubblicarla, non
senza le dovute sue illustrazioni, unitamente
alla Vita Nuova, alle Rime, al Convito, e all'

a

The family of Moderns (a relative term) in use today is extensive. One of the most misused of type styles (in text it needs plenty of leading), it can none the less, if handled with care, be highly effective. The major type in this group, Bodoni, exists in many versions of varying quality. Supplied by most founders, there are two basic versions : one from ATF by M. F. Benton (1907), which is virtually identical with the Monotype 135 version of 1921 and was based on a type in Bodoni's Manuale Tipografico. The second version is that of Bauer (1926, Heinrich Jost) and is more delicate. A third version – text sizes only – is

Monotype's *Bodoni Book* (1932), derived from founder's type. Although the letters below appear a little coarse, this is only because of their greater enlargement (from 12pt). They are, in fact, more delicate even than Bauer's, as can be seen in the full alphabets. Monotype's *Didot* of 1908 was derived from Firmin Didot's types from 1784 onwards, and Ludwig and Mayer's *Firmin Didot* also closely follows the originals, being recut from eighteenth-century drawings which survive and from printed specimens. (Deberny & Peignot hold the original punches.)

Berthold's *Walbaum* was cast from the original matrices of Justus Erich Walbaum, *c.* 1800, which were acquired by the foundry in 1919. The Monotype version (1933) is also virtually a facsimile with its pleasant irregularities particularly clear in smaller sizes, a feature which makes it a more sympathetic text type than the harsher Bodonis. The difference can be clearly seen here between a founder's type and a type for machine composition. The harder metal of founder's type allows greater delicacy and finer hairlines in the design of the letterforms.

RQENbaegn *baegn*

Enlarged from
30pt Bauer Bodoni

RQENbaegn *baegn*

Enlarged from
30pt Monotype 135 Bodoni

RQENbaegn *baegn*

Enlarged from
12pt Monotype 357 Bodoni Book

RQENbaegn
baegn

RQENbaegn
baegn

RQENbaegn
baegn

RQENbaegn
baegn

Extended 3 is probably a Victorian survival; *Modern Extended* (1902) is from a Miller & Richard face (probably cut by Richard Austin) which was used by *The Times*, and has a large number of mathematical and other signs – the former alone number over 600 sorts. *Modern 20* is derived from a number of faces, mostly cut by Stephenson Blake in the late nineteenth century.

RQENb
aegn

Enlarged from
24pt Stevens Shanks Extended 3

RQENbaegn
baegn

Enlarged from
12pt Monotype 7 Modern Extended

RQENbaegn
baegn

Enlarged from
30pt Stephenson Blake Modern 20

ABCDEFGHIJKLMNOPQRSTUVWXYZ
abcdefghijklmnopqrstuvwxyzæœffffifl
&ÆŒ£1234567890..;:-!?''()

ABCDEFGHIJKLMNOPQRSTUVWXYZ
abcdefghijklmnopqrstuvwxyzæœfffifl
&ÆŒ£1234567890..;:-!?''()

30pt Bauer Bodoni

ABCDEFGHIJKLMNOPQRSTUVWXYZ
abcdefghijklmnopqrstuvwxyzæœfffififlffiffl
&ÆŒ£1234567890..;:-!?''()

ABCDEFGHIJKLMNOPQRSTUVWXYZ
abcdefghijklmnopqrstuvwxyzæœfffififlffiffl
ÆŒ&£1234567890..;:-!?''()

30pt Monotype 135 Bodoni

ABCDEFGHIJKLMNOPQRSTUVWXYZ
abcdefghijklmnopqrstuvwxyzæœfffiflfififfl
&ÆŒ£1234567890.,:;-!?''()

12pt Monotype 357 Bodoni Book

ABCDEFGHIJKLMNOPQRSTUVWXYZ
abcdefghijklmnopqrstuvwxyzæœfff-fififfl
&ÆŒ£1234567890.,:;-!?''()

ABCDEFGHIJKLMNOPQRSTUVWXYZ
abcdefghijklmnopqrstuvwxyzæœfffiflfiffiffl
&ÆŒ£1234567890.,:;-!?''()

13pt Monotype 71 Didot

ABCDEFGHIJKLMNOPQRSTUVWXYZ
abcdefghijklmnopqrstuvwxyzæœfffiflfiffiffl
&ÆŒ.,:;-!?'

ABCDEFGHIJKLMNOPQRSTUVWXYZ
abcdefghijklmnopqrstuvwxyzæœfffififlfififlft
&ÆŒ£1234567890.,:;-!?'""()

ABCDEFGHIJKLMNOPQRSTUVWXYZ
abcdefghijklmnopqrstuvwxyzæœ
&ÆŒ1234567890.,:;-!?'""()

30pt large Ludwig & Mayer Firmin Didot

ABCDEFGHIJKLMNOPQRSTUVWXYZ
abcdefghijklmnopqrstuvwxyzæœfffifl
&ÆOE£1234567890.,;:-!?"()
ABCDEFGHIJKLMNOPQRSTUVWXYZ
abcdefghijklmnopqrstuvwxyzæœfffifl
&ÆOE£1234567890.,;:-!?"()

30D Berthold Walbaum

ABCDEFGHIJKLMNOPQRSTUVWXYZ
abcdefghijklmnopqrstuvwxyzæœfffiflffiffl
&ÆOE£1234567890.,;:-!?"()
ABCDEFGHIJKLMNOPQRSTUVWXYZ
abcdefghijklmnopqrstuvwxyzæœfffiflffiffl
&ÆOE1234567890.,;:-!?"()

30D on 36pt Monotype 374 Walbaum

ABCDEFGHIJKLMNOPQRST
UVWXYZ
abcdefghijklmnopqrstuvwxyzæœ fifl fffifffi ffl
&ÆOE£$1234567890,;:.-'!?

24pt Stevens Shanks Extended 3

ABCDEFGHIJKLMNOPQRSTUVWXYZ
abcdefghijklmnopqrstuvwxyzæœffflfiffifffl
&ÆOE£1234567890.,:;-!?"()

12pt Monotype 7 Modern Extended

ABCDEFGHIJKLMNOPQRSTUVWXYZ
abcdefghijklmnopqrstuvwxyzæœfffififfifl
&ÆOE.,:;-!?"()

ABCDEFGHIJKLMNOPQRSTUVWXYZ
abcdefghijklmnopqrstuvwxyzfffififlffiffl
&£1234567890.,;:-!?"
ABCDEFGHIJKLMNOPQRSTUVWXYZ
abcdefghijklmnopqrstuvwxyzæœfffififlffiffl
&ÆOE£1234567890.,;:-!?"()

30pt Stephenson Blake Modern 20

By exaggerating the strong verticals of Didot and Bodoni still further, founders supplied a new kind of face to feed the appetite of the Industrial Revolution for a punchy display alphabet for jobbing work. From the mid-eighteenth century onwards, gothic types or standard roman founts in a large size had been used for advertisements and posters, but they had hardly more impact than a bold title page. The new types thus marked a new era and the beginning of a new industry; and

the two handbills on this page show how a small provincial printer took up the challenge. John Soulby senior of Ulverston-in-Furness had a limited stock of Transitional roman types from Fry's foundry, which he used in the Baskerville manner. His son, John Soulby junior, acquired Fatface, Fatface Black and Egyptian types from the Bower and Bacon foundry and used them in a new manner: direct, economical and forceful.

Top: John Soulby senior. Ulverston, 1809. Barrow-in-Furness Public Library.

Bottom: John Soulby junior. Ulverston, 1833. Museum of English Rural Life, University of Reading.

Sold by J. SOULBY, Bookseller, ULVERSTONE,

A Beautiful Pink Stain,

FOR SILK STOCKINGS,

Price 1s. Per Bottle.

DIRECTIONS FOR USING IT.

FIRST, wash the Stockings you wish to stain, mix 3 tea spoon full of the Liquid in the Bottle with 3 pints of warm Water, keep putting the Stockings in and out of the Liquid alternately for ten or twelve Minutes which will stain them a beautiful Pink Colour;—put them through a Soap Lather and dry them betwixt a Flannel, or Cloth

N. B. If the Stockings be too light, add a little more of the Liquid out of the Bottle.

J. Soulby, Printer, Ulverstone.

DRIFTED

FROM

Conishead Bank,

NEAR ULVERSTON.

On SUNDAY, the 11th. Inst.

6 Baltic Pine BALKS,

Each Marked I. W. at one end with white Paint;

12 SPARS,

Marked N. with a Number.

Persons who will have the goodness to secure them will have all resonable expences paid, and be rewarded by Messrs. Petty and Co. Ulverston, who will prosecute with severity, any one detected secreting any of the property.

Ulverston, 13th, May, 1823,

John Soulby, Printer, Market Place, Ulverston.

The first fat face was issued by the founders Bower & Bacon in 1810. Its ancestor is the Modern letter of Bodoni ; later it was further developed in italic outline, three-dimensional and decorated forms. Similarly gothic types were weighted to give display letters of comparable punch.

The first truly original design of advertising type appeared in 1817 when Vincent Figgins brought out the first Egyptian face, which with its slab serifs and sledge-hammer even weight has been described as a typical expression of the new age. In the year 1814, *The Times*
was first produced on a steam press and the new technology found a matching typographical expression in these designs. Letters were no longer mere symbols for sounds but abstract shapes of compelling power which could not be ignored. The new typography which relied on a single word to get the attention of the passer-by demanded impact rather than legibility from the type-face. The heavy Egyptians are uncomfortable to read in small sizes and the 'fats' scarcely better, but as these Thorowgood specimens of 1828 show, big Egyptians whether caps or lower case are shapes to reckon with.

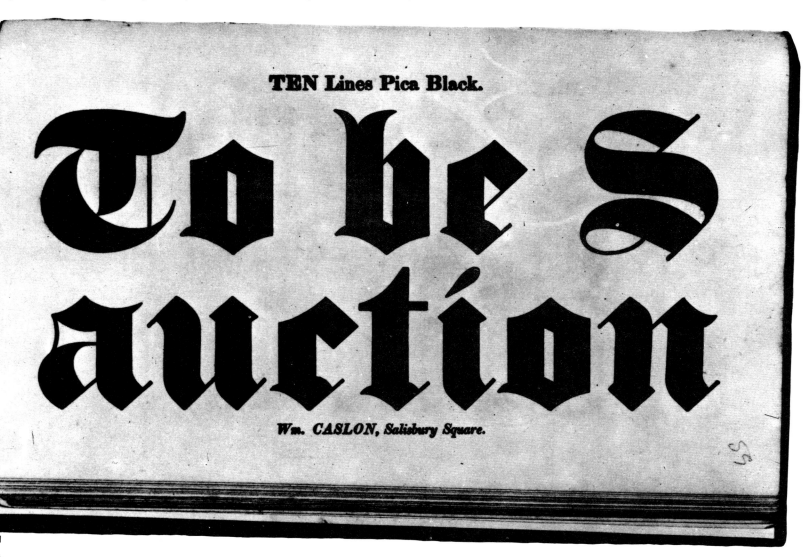

1

2

1. Blake Garnett : type specimen, 1819.
St Bride Printing Library, London.
2, 3 and 4. Thorowgood : type specimen, 1828.
St Bride Printing Library, London.

14 LINE EGYPTIAN.

MEN

THOROWGOOD, LATE THORNE, LONDON.

3
4

14 LINE EGYPTIAN.

main

THOROWGOOD, LATE THORNE, LONDON.

As with all styles, finer design points make a great difference to the fat-face group. *Ultra Bodoni* (1936) is a fat-face version of Monotype 135 ; unlike the Haas or Bauer ultra bolds, the junction of thick and thin strokes is abrupt. Even these aggressive forms are all the better for a little subtlety ; notice the merging junctions of *Falstaff* (1935), which in this respect is more like the Haas ultra bold, though bolder still, and nearer to the original fat-face form. The other two examples on this page also have the added richness and warmth that curving junctions give. *Thorowgood Italic,* revived from the

matrices of 1810 (perhaps those of Thorne), is in its original form. A roman was revived in 1953, after the italic, but unfortunately soon withdrawn owing to lack of demand ; it was rather similar to Falstaff, though a little richer in its curves. *Normande* (1931) follows originals of the early nineteenth century and was first cut in 1860.

Enlarged from
30pt Monotype 120 Bodoni Ultrabold

Enlarged from
30D on 36pt Monotype 323 Falstaff

Enlarged from
30pt Stephenson Blake Thorowgood Italic

Enlarged from
30pt Berthold Normande

ABCDEFGHIJKLMNOPQRSTUVWXYZ
abcdefghijklmnopqrstuvwxyzæœ
fiflffffiffl&ÆŒ£1234567890.,:;-!?"''()
ABCDEFGHIJKLMNOPQRSTUVW
XYZabcdefghijklmnopqrstuvwxyzæœ
fiflffffiffl&ÆŒ£1234567890.,:;-!?"''()

30pt Monotype 120 Bodoni Ultrabold

ABCDEFGHIJKLMNOPQRSTUV
WXYZabcdefghijklmnopqrstuv
wxyzæœfffififlffffiffl
&ÆŒ£1234567890.,:;-!?"''()
ABCDEFGHIJKLMNOPQRSTU
VWXYZabcdefghijklmnopqrstu
vwxyzæœfiflffffiffl
&ÆŒ£1234567890.,:;-!?"''()

30D on 36pt Monotype 323 Falstaff

ABCDEFGHIJKLMNOPQRSTUV
WXYZ.A.M.N.V.W
abcdefghijklmnopqrstuvwxyzæœ
&ŒÆ£1234567890.,:;-!?"'(

30pt Stephenson Blake Thorowgood Italic

ABCDEFGHIJKLMNOPQRSTUVWX
YZabcdefghijklmnopqrstuvwxyzæœ
&ÆŒ£1234567890.,:;-!?"'()
ABCDEFGHIJKLMNOPQRSTUVW
XYZabcdefghijklmnopqrstuvwxyzæœ
fffifflft&ÆŒ£1234567890.,:;-!?"''()

30pt Berthold Normande

This spread of Egyptians clearly shows the characteristics of this family. Many of them are originals; for instance, *Antique 6* (*c.* 1860) is from the Figgins foundry, since acquired by Stevens Shanks. Its irregularities and its changes of design from size to size (see alphabets) are typical of its period. Like many types from Stevens Shanks, these forms are the unmodified originals; but *Egyptian Bold Extended* (1955, Walter H. McKay), a modern design, has been regularized. *Egyptian Bold Condensed* is an anonymous nineteenth-century design, purer than most, and interesting to compare with *Superba Bold* (1928–30, E. Thiele) which has a more Germanic look. *Expanded Antique* (*c.* 1880) also came from Figgins. *Egyptian Expanded* (*c.* 1850) is a Miller & Richard face bought by Stephenson Blake *c.*1950. *Antique 5* (*c.*1860) is of similar origin to Antique 6; *Bold Latin Condensed* (*c.*1884–90) is a Victorian original revived soon after 1928 as a result of an article in *The Fleuron*. It has typical Stephenson Blake tuck-ins to the c and e, etc. It is not cast from the original matrices, but has been newly engraved with slight adjustments. With its triangular serifs, it displays the characteristics of a sub-section of Egyptians, called Latins.

Enlarged from
24pt Stevens Shanks Antique 6

Enlarged from
36pt Amsterdam Egyptian Bold Extended

Enlarged from
36pt Amsterdam Egyptian Bold Condensed

Enlarged from
28D Haas Superba Bold

RQEN

Enlarged from
18pt Stevens Shanks Expanded Antique

RQE
baeg

Enlarged from
30pt Stephenson Blake Egyptian Expanded

RQENbaegn

Enlarged from
30pt Stevens Shanks Antique 5

RQENbaegn

Enlarged from
30pt Stephenson Blake Bold Latin Condensed

These three types show how letterforms can be distorted, while retaining the family features. Highly condensed, and with reversed stress – horizontal instead of vertical – they are yet grouped with Egyptians. *Playbill* (1938) was suggested by Robert Harling and was modified from a Victorian wood letter. *Figaro* (1940) – in some ways a better form – is less Victorian in feeling. *Barnum* was originally issued by Barnhardt Bros. & Spindler in the nineteenth century.

RQEN baegn

Enlarged from
36pt Stephenson Blake Playbill

RQEN baegn

Enlarged from
36pt Monotype 536 Figaro

RQENbaegn

Enlarged from
30pt ATF Barnum

ABCDEFGHIJKLMNOPQR
STUVWXYZabcdefghijklm
nopqrstuvwxyzæœfiflffffifl
&ÆŒ£1234567890,;:.-'!?

ABCDEFGHIJKLMNOPQRSTUVWXYZ
abcdefghijklmnopqrstuvwxyzæœfiflffffifl
&ÆŒ£1234567890,;:.-'!?(

36pt and 24pt Stevens Shanks Antique 6

ABCDEFGHIJKLMNOPQR
STUVWXYZæœ
abcdefghijklmnopqrstuvwxyz
&ÆŒ£1234567890.,;:-!?"'()

36pt Amsterdam Egyptian Bold Extended

ABCDEFGHIJKLMNOPQRSTUVWXYZ
abcdefghijklmnopqrstuvwxyzæœ
&ÆŒ£1234567890.,;:-!?"'()

36pt Amsterdam Egyptian Bold Condensed

ABCDEFGHIJKLMNOPQRSTUVWXYZ
abcdefghijklmnopqrstuvwxyzæœ
&ÆŒ1234567890.,;:-!?'„"()

28D Haas Superba Bold

ABCDEFGHIJKL
MNOPQRSTUVWXYZ
&ÆŒ£1234567890,;:.-'Y

18pt Stevens Shanks Expanded Antique

ABCDEFGHIJK
LMNOPQRSTUV
WXYZ
abcdefghijklmno
pqrstuvwxyzæœ
ffffffffffff&ÆŒ£Ʒ
1234567890.,;:-!?""()

30pt Stephenson Blake Egyptian Expanded

ABCDEFGHIJKLMNOPQRSTUVWXYZ
abcdefghijklmnopqrstuvwxyzæœfiflffffiffl
&ÆŒ£1234567890,,;:.-'!?(

30pt Stevens Shanks Antique 5

ABCDEFGHIJKLMNOPQRSTUVWXYZ
abcdefghijklmnopqrstuvwxyzæœffffffffiffl
&ÆŒ£1234567890.,.:;-!?"()

30pt Stephenson Blake Bold Latin Condensed

ABCDEFGHIJKLMNOPQRSTUVWXYZ
abcdefghijklmnopqrstuvwxyzæœ
&ÆŒ£1234567890.,;:!?-""""[]

36pt Stephenson Blake Playbill

ABCDEFGHIJKLMNOPQRSTUVWXYZ
abcdefghijklmnopqrstuvwxyzæœ
&ÆŒ£1234567890.,:,!?-''()

36pt Monotype 536 Figaro

ABCDEFGHIJKLMNOPQRSTUVWXYZ
abcdefghijklmnopqrstuvwxyzfiflffffiffl
&$1234567890.,;:-!?"

30pt ATF Barnum

The Clarendons or Ionics which first appeared in the 1840's were a polite reaction to the fat faces and Egyptians. The forms of both caps and lower case were better proportioned, the serifs bracketed and the exaggeration toned down. These types had a very great success and still have, but their greatest importance lies in the use they are put to in their smaller sizes. Their 'normal'-looking yet solid and open shapes make them excellent for rough printing on poor quality paper, and today most faces for printing the text of newspapers (as well as faces for typewriters) are of the Clarendon group.

In terms of sheer quantity of words printed daily, Clarendon must be the most useful typeface ever invented. Again, many of those in use today are the original design, as is *Antique 3* of *c.*1860 – another type from V. and J. Figgins originals. *Clarendon* (1903) is only available in text sizes; Monotype *Ionic* (1932) – also text sizes only – is, unlike most Ionics, suitable for general printing as well as newspapers; Clarendon (series 12) is a useful bold.

Century Schoolbook (1924, M. F. Benton) is derived from the original design of *c.*1890 by L. B. Benton for

the *Century* magazine. The Monotype version (1934) is used in the text setting at the back of this atlas; display sizes of modified design (series 650), somewhat similar to the ATF version, were brought out in 1964 for *The Observer* newspaper.

RQEN baegn

Enlarged from
30pt Stevens Shanks Antique 3

RQENbaegn

Enlarged from
12pt Monotype 12 Clarendon

RQENbaeg
n *baegn*

Enlarged from
9pt Monotype 342 Ionic

RQENbaegn *baegn*

Enlarged from
30pt ATF Century Schoolbook

The Clarendons shown here are typical of many founders. *Consort* light and normal (1956–7) were revived from Reed's extended Clarendon, cut by Fox – Charles Reed's partner – and registered in 1845. The bold (1956–7) is a new design. The forms get progressively coarser as the weight increases : the light is particularly delicate and sensitive. The Haas and Stempel versions (1951–3, H. Eidenbenz) are the same design, with a wide range of weights : apart from those shown, there is a semi-bold and a light condensed.

RQENbaegn
RQENbaegn

Enlarged from
30pt Stephenson Blake Consort Condensed and Light Condensed

RQENbae
gn

Enlarged from
30pt Stephenson Blake Consort Bold

RQENbae
gn

Enlarged from
30pt Stephenson Blake Consort

RQENbae
gn

Enlarged from
30pt Stephenson Blake Consort Light

RQEN
baegn
Enlarged from
28D Haas (Stempel) Clarendon Bold Expanded

RQENbae
gn
Enlarged from
28D Haas (Stempel) Clarendon Bold

RQENbae
gn
Enlarged from
28D Haas (Stempel) Clarendon Medium

RQENbae
gn
Enlarged from
28D Haas (Stempel) Clarendon Light

ABCDEFGHIJKLMNOPQRSTUVWXYZ
abcdefghijklmnopqrstuvwxyzæœfiflffffiffl
&ÆŒ£1234567890,;:.-'!?([

30pt Stevens Shanks Antique 3

ABCDEFGHIJKLMNOPQRSTUVWXYZ
abcdefghijklmnopqrstuvwxyzæœffflfiffiffl
&ÆŒ£1234567890.,:;-!?''()
ABCDEFGHIJKLMNOPQRSTUVWXYZ
abcdefghijklmnopqrstuvwxyzæœfflflfiffiffl
&ÆŒ£1234567890.,:;-!?''()

9pt Monotype 342 Ionic

ABCDEFGHIJKLMNOPQRSTUVWXYZ
abcdefghijklmnopqrstuvwxyzæœfflflfiffiffl
&ÆŒ£1234567890.,:;-!?''()

12pt Monotype 12 Clarendon

ABCDEFGHIJKLMNOPQRSTUVWXYZ
abcdefghijklmnopqrstuvwxyzfiffflffifffl
&$1234567890.,-:;!?"
ABCDEFGHIJKLMNOPQRSTUVWXYZ
abcdefghijklmnopqrstuvwxyzfiffflffifffl
&$1234567890.,-:;!?"''

30pt ATF Century Schoolbook

ABCDEFGHIJKLMNOPQRSTUVWXYZ
abcdefghijklmnopqrstuvwxyzæœfiflffffiffl
&ÆŒ£1234567890.,:;-!?''()
ABCDEFGHIJKLMNOPQRSTUVWXYZ
abcdefghijklmnopqrstuvwxyzæœfiflffffiffl
&ÆŒ£1234567890.,:;-!?''()

30pt Monotype 650 Century

ABCDEFGHIJKLMNOPQRSTUVWXYZ
abcdefghijklmnopqrstuvwxyzæœffififlffiffl
&ÆŒ£1234567890.,:;!?-'()
ABCDEFGHIJKLMNOPQRSTUVWXYZ
abcdefghijklmnopqrstuvwxyzæœffflfiflffiffl
&ÆŒ£1234567890.,:;!?-''()

30pt Stephenson Blake Consort Condensed and Light Condensed

ABCDEFGHIJKLMNOPQRSTUVW
XYZabcdefghijklmnopqrstuvwxyz
fffiflffiffl&£1234567890.,;:-!?"

ABCDEFGHIJKLMNOPQRSTUVWXYZ
abcdefghijklmnopqrstuvwxyzæœfffififlffiffi
&ÆŒ£1234567890.,;:!?-'()

ABCDEFGHIJKLMNOPQRSTUVW
XYZabcdefghijklmnopqrstuvwxyz
fffififlffiffi&£1234567890.,;:-!?"

30pt Stephenson Blake Consort Bold, Medium and Light

ABCDEFGHIJKLMNOPQ
RSTUVWXYZabcdefghij
klmnopqrstuvwxyz
&1234567890.,-:;!?'()„"»«/—[]

28D Haas (Stempel) Clarendon Bold Expanded

ABCDEFGHIJKLMNOPQRSTUVWX
YZabcdefghijklmnopqrstuvwxyzæœ
fifl&ÆŒ1234567890.,;:-!?',"()

ABCDEFGHIJKLMNOPQRSTUVWXZ
abcdefghijklmnopqrstuvwxyzæœfifl Y
&ÆŒ1234567890.,;:-!?',"()

ABCDEFGHIJKLMNOPQRSTUVWXYZ
abcdefghijklmnopqrstuvwxyzæœfffifl
&ÆŒ£1234567890.,-:;!?'()„"»«/—§†*

28D Haas (Stempel) Clarendon Bold, Medium and Light

The fats and slabs dominated ephemeral printing of the early nineteenth century and, together with sans-serif faces which are discussed later, are as much the proper study of the twentieth-century typographer as the old subtle roman types with their long and intricate history. Display types of the early kind formed a foundation for a host of developments during the nineteenth century and modern designers constantly draw on the stock of astonishingly inventive designs of the Victorians. Display alphabets date back to the Roman inscriptions ; *Union Pearl* (p.95) was cut before 1700 ; we have shown an example of

Fournier's open roman of 1764 ; but these are only isolated forerunners of the great families of display faces that appeared in the middle years of the nineteenth century. The first of these were variations on the designs of fat face and Egyptian like the examples from the 1820's and 1830's shown on this page. During the next decade further decorated, outline, shadow or three-dimensional types appeared. Tuscans, with leafy or fruity explosions in place of serifs, and Latins, with serifs in the form of severe wedges, gave the jobbing printers of the 1840's and 1850's shapes which they used with equal boldness

and invention. The Astley's circus poster shows a typical example of the 1840's. Towards the end of the century display faces became more intricate and genteel, lighter in weight and more self-conscious.

Type encyclopaedias show hundreds of modern display types and the reader should turn to them for a comprehensive showing ; on the next spread a small collection is shown of complete alphabets to give some idea of the variety available to the designer. Many are nineteenth-century designs, as during that century a large number of the best and most inventive types were cut.

SIX LINE REVERSED EGYPTIAN ITALIC,

HOMERTON
MOLDER

THOROWGOOD, LONDON.

1
2

FOUR LINE PICA ORNAMENTED.

MANCHESTER
£278000.

CANON ORNAMENTED.

FINSBURY PLACE.
Mrs. £123456

THOROWGOOD, LONDON.

By the 1880's display types were needed in great quantities for press advertising, and their design altered accordingly to suit the reduced scale. But at the turn of the twentieth century the influence of *art nouveau* inspired original designs which have lately returned to favour.

1. Thorowgood: type specimen, 1828.
St Bride Printing Library, London.
2. Thorowgood: type specimen, 1834.
St Bride Printing Library, London.

3. Klatt Benefit; Astley's Bill, 1845.
Enthoven Collection. Victoria and Albert Museum, London.

ABCDEFGHIJKLMNOPQR
STUVWXYZÆŒ.,'::-

Enschedé Rosart

ABCDEFGHIJKLMNOPQRST
UVWXYZ&1234567890.,:;'-!9()""

28D Nebiolo Augustea Filettata

ABCDEFGHIJKLMNOPQRSTUVW
XYZ&£1234567890.,:;-!?'

36pt Stephenson Blake Sans Serif Shaded

ABCDEFGHIJKLMNOPQRSTUV
WXYZ&$£1234567890.,-:;!?'()»«

28D Weber Forum II

ABCDEFGHIJKLMNOPQRSTUVWXYZ
&£1234567890.,:;-!?'

24pt Stephenson Blake Thorne Shaded

ABCDEFGHIJKLMNOPQRSTUVWXYZ
1234567890.,:-!

Deberny & Peignot Lettres Ombrées

ABCDEFGHIJKLMNOPQRSTUVWXY

30D Olive Calypso

ABCDEFGHIJKLMNOPQRSTU
VWXYZabcdefghijklmnopqrs
tuvwxyz&1234567890$.,-:;!?'{}

36pt ATF Cooper Hilite

ABCDEFGHIJKLMNOPQRSTUVW
XYZ&$¢1234567890.,:;-!?"

30pt ATF Stencil

ABCDEFGHIJKLMNOPQRSTUVWXYZ
&ÆŒ1234567890.,;:-!?'«»()

14pt Haas Chevalier

ABCDEFGHIJKLMNOPQRSTUVWXYZ
abcdefghijklmnopqrstuvwxyz . , & ſt ß ſ ð y Qu

22pt Stephenson Blake Union Pearl

ABCDEFGHIJKLMNOPQ
RSTUVWXYZ~
1234567890.,;:-!?

36pt ATF Modernistic

ABCDEFGHIJKLMNOPQRSTUVWXYZ
abcdefghijklmnopqrstuvwxyzæœfifl ff
&ÆŒ£1234567890.,;:!?-""()

24pt Monotype 442 Gill Sans Ultrabold

ABCDEFGHIJKLMNOPQRSTUVWXYZ
abcdefghijklmnopqrstuvwxyzæœ ff ffi fl
&ÆŒ£1234567890.,;:-!?""()

30pt Bauer Futura Black

ABCDEFGHIJKLMNOPQRSTU
VWXYZ
&ÆŒ£1234567890.,;:-!?""()

36pt Deberny & Peignot Bifur

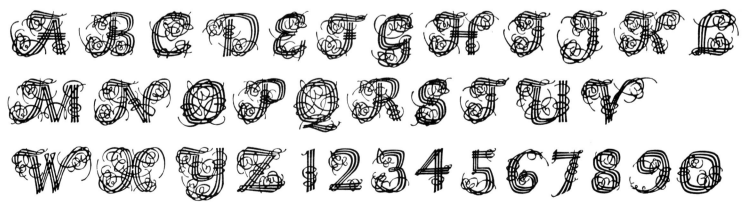

42D on 48pt Amsterdam Raffia Initials

stitute in these the principal lines, for which nothing larger than pica should be used. In running on matter, the lighter it is set and the better. When borders round the job would improve its appearance, taste only can decide.

HAND-BILLS AND POSTERS

Belong to a rougher description of work, in which neatness yields to propriety and taste to effect. In hand-bills and posters, the large lines are made to read on with each other, so that the substance may be read at a glance. Any other particulars are only considered secondary lines, and are set small or large, according to their apparent import. Catch lines, which are merely used to connect one line with another, are always set small, in capitals or small capitals. The following advertisement will perhaps illustrate the principle.

TO BE SOLD,
BY PRIVATE TREATY,
A BEAUTIFUL FOUR-WHEELED
PHAETON,
A FINE WELL-BRED
MARE,
About 14½ hands high, warranted sound, is very steady, and trots very fast,
AND
HARNESS COMPLETE.

Apply at, &c., &c.

In the above example, To be Sold—Phaeton—Mare—and Harness Complete, are principal lines, and would be perfectly understood without any other word; hence they are the largest, that they may be readily seen. By Private Treaty—About fourteen and a half hands high, &c.—are secondary-lines, or what would only be looked for if there were any desire to purchase. A beautiful four-wheeled—

a fine well-bred—and—are catch-lines, because they are merely used to connect the lines and to make them read smoothly. Apply, &c.—partakes more of the nature of a note, and hence the reason for being always cut off with a rule, and run on in smaller type. It is of little consequence what may be the size of the bill, whether for the hand or the wall, the *principle* which points out the leading and secondary lines is still the same.

In setting bills, then, set the principal lines first, that the effect may be judged of, and the remaining space for the other lines may be determined. After which fill up the bill in hand with its secondary and catch lines. By doing so, the necessity for altering lines to get in, may be avoided. If you would set a bill expeditiously, determine *at once* what letter will do for *the* line wanted, and avoid, by all means, setting the line again. It is unnecessary, and often consumes more time than would be required to set the bill twice over. Altering one line often requires an alteration of another, or two, which after all may make the bill no better than at first. This is the principal secret of setting a bill quick, and not picking up a great number of letters in a little time, though this, indeed, may facilitate it.

TABLE WORK

Includes every description of rule-work, whether the space between the rules contains matter or not, and comprehends all that is distinguished in the trade by rule-work, tabular, or tables. This is the most difficult description of work, inasmuch as every job belonging to it requires great accuracy, both in the length of rules and in justifying. So much so, indeed, that the time which such-like jobs consume, is considered worth double the amount of common matter, and is paid for accordingly. There is, however, a great difference in the method of setting this description of work; but I will confine myself to that method which I think is not generally known, and which appears to save the most time. In this system all the columns are set across, instead, as is usual, of

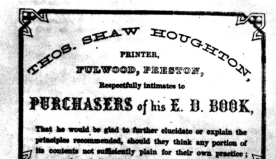

THOS. SHAW HOUGHTON,
PRINTER,
FULWOOD, PRESTON,
Respectfully intimates to
PURCHASERS of his E. D. BOOK,
That he would be glad to further elucidate or explain the principles recommended, should they think any portion of its contents not sufficiently plain for their own practice; *correspondents finding the necessary postage stamps.*

In the above example, it will be seen that, though the lines vary in size, the thickness of all bear a uniform proportion to each, which makes the whole contrast agreeably and consistently. Each line is plain and distinct, and looks better and neater than a thick heavy line could do however placed.

SECTION IV.—TABULAR.

TABULAR-WORK is any description of matter classified and arranged in separate columns to read across the page, and embraces all lists, registers, &c., &c. It has a strong resemblance to both column matter and table-work, yet it essentially differs from both. Like column-work it consists of common set matter; but that is all, for here the likeness ceases, as column matter reads down one column at once, and tabular reads across the columns and makes the last line of the first the last of all. And in doing so and being generally printed with column-headings, it is like table-work, but with this difference, that tabular consists principally of ordinary matter, but tables, of figures. Tabular, therefore, can never become table-work, under any circumstance; nor can it ever be column matter, even without headings. The

number of columns only regulate the compositor's charge both for this and column matter, but does not change its nature.

Tabular is adapted to various kinds of subjects and always with the view of saving space and of improving the form and appearance of the work. Its columns may be without rules or headings but such is not the common practice. The number of columns vary, and may consist of twenty. as well as three ; and the matter turn over promiscuously in each, whatever be the number. This work always requires attention, the difficulty of setting it increasing in proportion to the nature of the matter and the number of the columns depending upon each other. There are two ways of setting tabular—the one in one column at once, the other in several columns together.

The usual practice of the trade was formerly to set this kind of work in single columns, and to empty each on as many separate galleys as might be required; the making-up being left to the last, to ascertain in what columns the matter turned over, and where to insert white lines to make it read. The matter was then made-up column after column, and a rule inserted after each as every subsequent column was made to read with those which preceded it. I need not enumerate the many vexatious annoyances which frequently arise from this method of setting and making-up tabular work. Those who have had any experience on it well know what confusion and loss of time is occasioned in making-up, when a line out of one column and a line out of another, and one perhaps out of a third, in different parts of the matter, is discovered after a few pages of tabular have been made up and read. For myself, there is no kind of work with which I am more familiar than with this ; and I speak from my own knowledge when I say, that half-a-day or a day's work being entirely lost, and the matter being re-made-up through outs, doubles, and transpositions of lines and even of portions of columns, by this method of setting tabular-work, was an occurrence much more frequent than agreeable. Nor is this all, for many other things connected with it, of minor import, add their mite to the general stock of annoyance and loss of time.

This method of setting tabular was the only one I had seen or heard of during the whole of my apprenticeship, and until the year 1832, when I was placed in circumstances requiring me to superintend a heavy job, and to get out between seven and eight hundred foolscap folio pages of tabular-work in a few weeks. The many scources of

The founding of the Kelmscott Press, dedicated to reviving the highest standards of printing, led Morris to experiment with paper, ink and binding as well as commissioning illustrations from Burne-Jones and engraving rich borders. Morris also drew two original typefaces : *Golden*, inspired by Jenson's roman, and *Chaucer* (also named *Troy* in a larger size), based on fourteenth-century German manuscript forms. Neither type nor typography bears much relationship to modern practice, but Morris's achievements earned him devoted disciples whose own private press work at length forced the printing trade to improve standards.

The Golden Legend. Kelmscott Press, Hammersmith, 1892. Victoria and Albert Museum, London. William Morris's *Golden* type is a heavy roman based on Jenson's Venetian roman of 1470. But Morris was a medievalist anc his typography recalls dark manuscripts rather than the airy pages of Renaissance Venice.

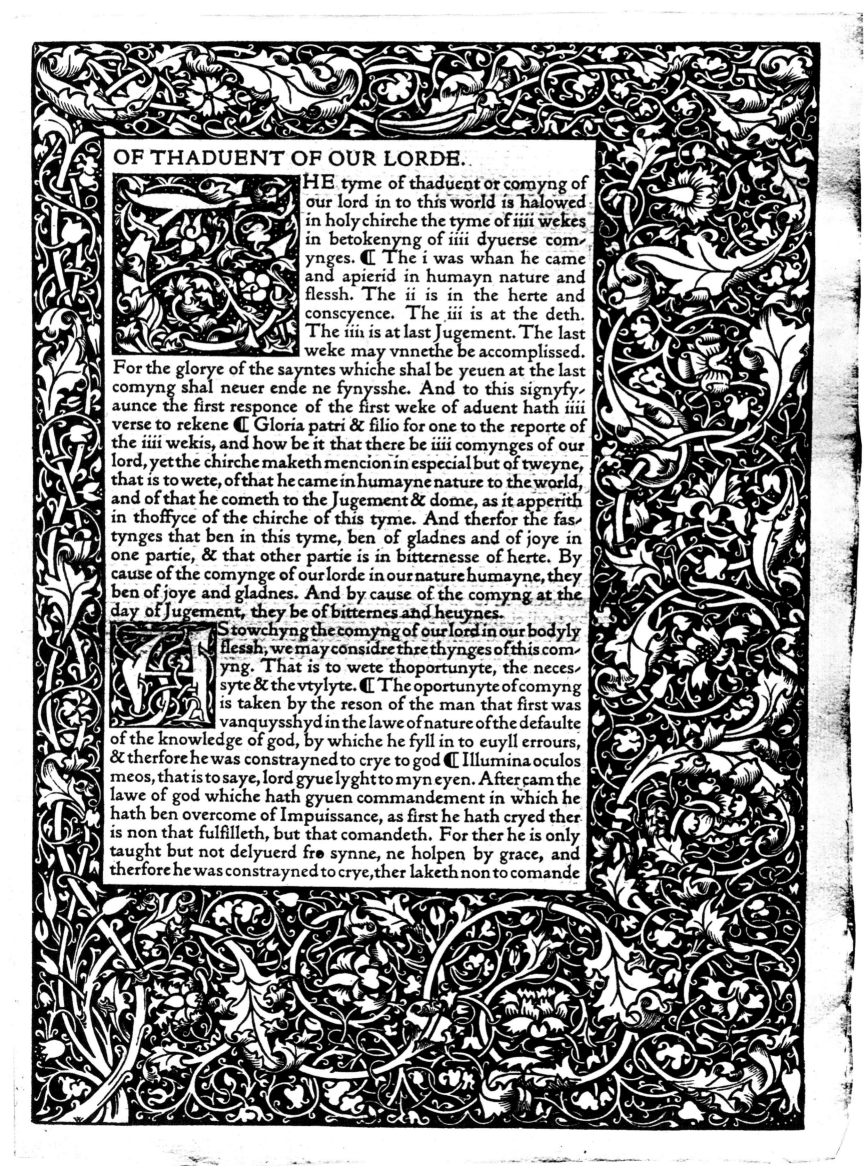

OF THADUENT OF OUR LORDE.

HE tyme of thaduent or comyng of our lord in to this world is halowed in holy chirche the tyme of iiii wekes in betokenyng of iiii dyuerse comynges. ℭ The i was whan he came and apierid in humayn nature and flessh. The ii is in the herte and conscyence. The iii is at the deth. The iiii is at last Jugement. The last weke may vnnethe be accomplissed. For the glorye of the sayntes whiche shal be yeuen at the last comyng shal neuer ende ne fynysshe. And to this signyfyaunce the first responce of the first weke of aduent hath iiii verse to rekene ℭ Gloria patri & filio for one to the reporte of the iiii wekis, and how be it that there be iiii comynges of our lord, yet the chirche maketh mencion in especial but of tweyne, that is to wete, of that he came in humayne nature to the world, and of that he cometh to the Jugement & dome, as it apperith in thoffyce of the chirche of this tyme. And therfor the fastynges that ben in this tyme, ben of gladnes and of joye in one partie, & that other partie is in bitternesse of herte. By cause of the comynge of our lorde in our nature humayne, they ben of joye and gladnes. And by cause of the comyng at the day of Jugement, they be of bitternes and heuynes.

S towchyng the comyng of our lord in our bodyly flessh, we may considre thre thynges of this comyng. That is to wete thoportunyte, the necessyte & the vtylyte. ℭ The oportunyte of comyng is taken by the reson of the man that first was vanquysshyd in the lawe of nature of the defaulte of the knowledge of god, by whiche he fyll in to euyll errours, & therfore he was constrayned to crye to god ℭ Illumina oculos meos, that is to saye, lord gyue lyght to myn eyen. After cam the lawe of god whiche hath gyuen commandement in which he hath ben overcome of Impuissance, as first he hath cryed ther is non that fulfilleth, but that comandeth. For ther he is only taught but not delyuerd fro synne, ne holpen by grace, and therfore he was constrayned to crye, ther laketh non to comande

These twentieth-century text types result from the private press revival. Design features are drawn from all families ; they are all original designs, often reflecting the individual style of a particular designer, not based on any particular historical example. National characteristics – for instance the living calligraphic tradition in Germany – are often reflected in the design. Their one common factor is that they are more Old Face in feeling than Modern.

Perpetua (1928, Eric Gill) is a translation into metal of Gill's sharply carved lettering, and still retains too much of this character for a good text type. Compare it with Garamond or Baskerville. It was not directly photographed and pantographed in the usual way, but was first cut by Charles Malin, of Paris ; matrices were struck, the type cast, and pulls made ; the final drawings were done from these. An influential, if rather chilly, type. *Joanna* (1930, Eric Gill) was originally intended for the designer's private press, Hague & Gill, and was cut by H. W. Caslon & Co. Ltd. The press was later bought up by J. M. Dent, who commissioned a machine composition version from Monotype in 1937. It was made generally available in 1958. Like Perpetua, t still retains too much stone-carved form for it to be really satisfactory as a type, which has a special need of rhythm and smoothness over long passages of text. Signwriting forms, carved forms and type forms are not usually interchangeable. *Pilgrim* (1953, Eric Gill) was originally designed for the Limited Editions Club, of New York, and called Bunyan, and is perhaps Gill's most satisfactory text type. *Emerson* (1930, Joseph Blumenthal) was originally cast from hand-cut punches

RQENbaegn
baegn

RQENbaegn
baegn

RQENbaegn
baegn

RQENbaegn
baegn

by Bauer, and called Spiral. The Monotype version was brought out in 1953. *Lutetia* (1926, Van Krimpen) was first cut by Enschedé ; a Monotype version, adapted by Van Krimpen, appeared in 1930. It has no obvious ancestors. *Romulus* (1931, Van Krimpen) also designed for Enschedé, with a Monotype version in 1936, again does not fit into traditional groupings of typeforms. It has a wide range of related weights and versions, including an undistinguished sans-serif, all mated and aligning. *Spectrum* (1941–3, Van Krimpen), another Enschedé

type, was designed originally (though not used) for a range of bibles, which accounts for certain features : smallish, narrow caps, narrowish lower case, large x-height. It was not actually cut until 1952, and was brought out by Monotype in 1955. It is in the Aldine tradition, with an italic based on the calligraphy of Arrighi. *Dante* (1954, Dr Giovanni Mardersteig) was designed by the director for the Officina Bodoni, which first used it in a hand-cut version by Charles Malin. It was faithfully adapted by Monotype in 1957–9.

RQENbaegn
baegn

Enlarged from
28D Monotype 255 Lutetia and 16D on 18pt Italic

RQENbaegn
baegn

Enlarged from
28D on 30pt Monotype 458 Romulus

RQENbaegn
baegn

Enlarged from
28D on 30pt Monotype 556 Spectrum

RQENbaegn
baegn

Enlarged from
14D on 16pt Monotype 592 Dante

Electra (1935–49, W. A. Dwiggins) is generally Old Face in character, though with flat serifs. *Caledonian* (1938, also by W. A. Dwiggins) is a modified Scotch Roman. *Juliana* (1958, S. L. Hartz) is a rather narrow, finely drawn bookface with a faint incline. *Diethelm* (1948–50, Walter Diethelm) is generally Old Face in feeling but with horizontal serifs. The next three are also German designs, showing a calligraphic influence but with rather square forms, quite unfamiliar in Britain. *Schadow* (1938–52, George Trump) has some Egyptian features though it is a finely designed roman type, while *Melior* (1952, Hermann Zapf) has hints of Modern. *Aldus* (1954, also by Zapf) is more Old Face in character; but the texture given to the page by these three types is quite different from that given by a Gill or Van Krimpen typeface.

Times (1932, 'excogitated', his own word, by Stanley Morison) drawn out by Victor Lardent at Printing House Square for *The Times*, is a very widely used type made by many founders although designed for its special purpose. There is a story, probably untrue, that a young designer talking to Morison suggested Plantin would make a good general text type if refined and sharpened. 'Quite true', replied Morison, 'and you'll get Times New Roman'.

Commercial considerations, such as economy and technical utility, were the governing factors in the introduction of most of the twentieth-century romans. Paradoxically, *Perpetua* which had great commercial success, was not designed in answer to a specific commercial problem.

Enlarged from
11pt Linotype (London) Electra

Enlarged from
14pt Linotype (London) Caledonia

Enlarged from
12pt Linotype (London) Juliana

Enlarged from
28D Haas Diethelm Roman

RQEN baegn
baegn

RQEN baegn
baegn

RQEN baegn
baegn

RQEN baegn
baegn

ABCDEFGHIJKLMNOPQRSTUVWXYZ
abcdefghijklmnopqrstuvwxyzæœfiflffffiffl
&ÆŒ£1234567890.,:;-!?''()
ABCDEFGHIJKLMNOPQRSTUVWXYZ
abcdefghijklmnopqrstuvwxyzæœfiflffffiffl
&ÆŒ£1234567890.,:;-!?''()

30pt Monotype 239 Perpetua

ABCDEFGHIJKLMNOPQRSTUVWXYZ
abcdefghijklmnopqrstuvwxyzæœfiflffffiffl
&ÆŒ£1234567890.,:;-!?''()
ABCDEFGHIJKLMNOPQRSTUVWXYZ
abcdefghijklmnopqrstuvwxyzæœfiflffffiffl
&ÆŒ£1234567890.,:;-!?''()

30pt Monotype 478 Joanna

ABCDEFGHIJKLMNOPQRSTUVWXYZ
abcdefghijklmnopqrstuvwxyzæœfiflffffiffl
£ÆŒ£1234567890.,:;-!?''()

14pt Linotype (London) Pilgrim and 10pt Italic

ABCDEFGHIJKLMNOPQRSTUVWXYZ
abcdefghijklmnopqrstuvwxyzæœfifl.ffiffl
&ÆŒ£123456789.,:;-!?''()

ABCDEFGHIJKLMNOPQRSTUVWXYZ
abcdefghijklmnopqrstuvwxyzæœfiflffffiffl
&ÆŒ£1234567890.,:;-!?''()
ABCDEFGHIJKLMNOPQRSTUVWXYZ
abcdefghijklmnopqrstuvwxyzæœfiflffffiffl
&ÆŒ1234567890.,:;-!?''

24pt Monotype 320 Emerson

ABCDEFGHIJKLMNOPQRSTUVWXYZ
abcdefghijklmnopqrstuvwxyzæœfiflffffiffl
&ÆŒ£1234567890.,:;-!?''()
ABCDEFGHIJKLMNOPQRSTUVWXYZ
abcdefghijklmnopqrstuvwxyzæœfiflffffiffl
&ÆŒ1234567890.,:;-!?''()

28D Monotype 255 Lutetia and 16D on 18pt Italic

ABCDEFGHIJKLMNOPQRSTUVWXYZ
abcdefghijklmnopqrstuvwxyzæœfiflfffffiffl
&ÆŒ£1234567890.,:;-!?"()
ABCDEFGHIJKLMNOPQRSTUVWXYZ
abcdefghijklmnopqrstuvwxyzæœfiflfffffiffl
&ÆŒ£1234567890.,:;-!?"()

28D on 30pt Monotype 458 Romulus

ABCDEFGHIJKLMNOPQRSTUVWXYZ
abcdefghijklmnopqrstuvwxyzæœfiflfffffiffl
&ÆŒ£1234567890.,:;-!?"()
ABCDEFGHIJKLMNOPQRSTUVWXYZ
abcdefghijklmnopqrstuvwxyzæœfiflfffffiffl
&ÆŒ£1234567890.,:;-!?"()

28D on 30pt Monotype 556 Spectrum

ABCDEFGHIJKLMNOPQRSTUVWXYZ
abcdefghijklmnopqrstuvwxyzæœffflfiffiffl
&ÆŒ£1234567890.,:;-!?"()

14D on 16pt Monotype 592 Dante

ABCDEFGHIJKLMNOPQRSTUVWXYZ
abcdefghijklmnopqrstuvwxyzæœffflfiffiffl
&ÆŒ£1234567890.,:;-!?"()

ABCDEFGHIJKLMNOPQRSTUVWXYZ
abcdefghijklmnopqrstuvwxyzæœfiflfffffiffl
&ÆŒ£1234567890.,;:-!?"()

11pt Linotype (London) Electra

ABCDEFGHIJKLMNOPQRSTUVWXYZ
abcdefghijklmnopqrstuvwxyzæœfiflfffffiffl
&ÆŒ£1234567890.,;:-!?"()

ABCDEFGHIJKLMNOPQRSTUVWXYZ
abcdefghijklmnopqrstuvwxyzæœfiflfffffiffl
&ÆŒ£1234567890.,;:-!?"()

14pt Linotype (London) Caledonia

ABCDEFGHIJKLMNOPQRSTUVWXYZ
abcdefghijklmnopqrstuvwxyzæœfiflffffiffl
&ÆŒ£1234567890.,;:-!?"()

ABCDEFGHIJKLMNOPQRSTUVWXYZ
abcdefghijklmnopqrstuvwxyzæœfiflfffffiffl
&ÆŒ£1234567890.,;:!?"()

12pt Linotype (London) Juliana

ABCDEFGHIJKLMNOPQRSTUVWXYZ
abcdefghijklmnopqrstuvwxyzæœfiflffffiffl
&ÆŒ£1234567890.,;:!?"()

ABCDEFGHIJKLMNOPQRSTUVWXYZ
abcdefghijklmnopqrstuvwxyzæœfifl
&ÆŒ1234567890.,;:-!?',„"()
ABCDEFGHIJKLMNOPQRSTUVWXYZ
abcdefghijklmnopqrstuvwxyzæœffffiflft
&ÆŒ1234567890.,;::-!?',„"()

28D Haas Diethelm Roman

ABCDEFGHIJKLMNOPQRSTUVWXYZ
abcdefghijklmnopqrstuvwxyz
&$£1234567890.,-;:!?'()»«·—/
ABCDEFGHIJKLMNOPQRSTUVWXYZ
abcdefghijklmnopqrstuvwxyz
&$£1234567890.,-;:!?'()»«·—/

28D Weber Schadow-Antiqua

ABCDEFGHIJKLMNOPQRSTUVWXYZ
abcdefghijklmnopqrstuvwxyzæœfffifl
&ÆŒ1234567890.,-:;!?()„"»«/–[]§†*
ABCDEFGHIJKLMNOPQRSTUVWXYZ
abcdefghijklmnopqrstuvwxyzæœfffifl
&ÆŒ1234567890.,-:;!?()„"»«/–[]§†

30pt Stempel Melior

ABCDEFGHIJKLMNOPQRSTUVWXYZ
abcdefghijklmnopqrstuvwxyz æœ ffififlft & ÆŒ
1234567890.,;:-!?''„"/·[]§—()

12pt Stempel Aldus

ABCDEFGHIJKLMNOPQRSTUVWXYZ
abcdefghijklmnopqrstuvwxyz fffiflft &
1234567890.,=:;"!?†§()[]'„"—*

ABCDEFGHIJKLMNOPQRSTUVWXYZ
abcdefghijklmnopqrstuvwxyzæœfiflfffffiffl
&ÆŒ£1234567890.,:;-!?"'()
ABCDEFGHIJKLMNOPQRSTUVWXYZ
abcdefghijklmnopqrstuvwxyzæœfiflfffffiffl
&ÆŒ£1234567890.,:;-!?''()

30pt Monotype 327 Times

We have seen that during the first twenty years of the nineteenth century, following the invention of the Modern letter by Didot and Bodoni, a number of entirely new display faces were produced to meet the demands of jobbing printers. For us today by far the most significant of these types made a modest first appearance in 1816 when the first sans-serif specimen was put out by the Caslon foundry. The new design looks timid and rather ungainly and was probably intended for sub-headings and short lines of texts under the shadow of the triumphant fats and slabs. For some time it was used in this way and was available in caps only. By the 1830's lower-case grotesques were in use in Germany, and soon afterwards in the USA, but not widely in Britain until the 1870's. By the end of the century every founder had a full range of grotesques (as sans-serif type had come to be known) ranging from light to ultra bold, condensed to expanded. This in fact was the greatest strength of the design.

Unlike romans, for example, grotesques could be designed in every imaginable way, related to each other, yet capable of use in the most varied circumstances. In the reaction against the nineteenth century during the first twenty-five years of this century, new versions of sans were designed to avoid the exuberance of the nineteenth-century forms. Gill's sans had great distinction and sensitive drawing, and Renner's Futura an impressive austere geometry, but today these have been overtaken by grotesques derived from nineteenth-century sources, with clean, sophisticated lines, carefully judged weights and proportions, and a comprehensive range of sizes to meet ever more exacting modern needs.

Here we show development from Caslon's 1816 type, via Victorian designs, to the refined Standard.

Two line English Egyptian

W CASLON JUNR   LETTERFOUNDER

Two line nonpareil, Sans-serif

A LARGE, AND ELEGANT ASSORTMENT, OF THE MOST MODERN JOB LETTER.
ABCDEFGHIJKLMNOPQRSTUVWX

Seven line Grotesque

MENINGHURNE
mountainous

30pt Stevens Shanks Royal Gothic

ABCDEFGHIJKLMNOPQRSTUVWXYZ
abcdefghijklmnopqrstuvwxyz
&£1234567890.,:;.?!"'()

30pt Berthold Standard Normal and Normal Series 57

ABCDEFGHIJKLMNOPQRSTUVWXYZ
abcdefghijklmnopqrstuvwxyz
&ÆŒ£1234567890.,;:-!?"()
ABCDEFGHIJKLMNOPQRSTUVWXYZ
abcdefghijklmnopqrstuvwxyzæœfffiflft
&ÆŒ£1234567890.,;:-!?"()

Johnston's Railway Type (1916, Edward Johnston) was commissioned by Frank Pick for the exclusive use of London's Underground and associated companies. The first of the twentieth-century sans, it is still used for all London Transport official signs and notices. The proportions are based on classical letterforms, and not those of nineteenth-century grotesques. *Gill Sans* (1928, Eric Gill) obviously owes much to the sans of the designer's friend and teacher, Johnston. The forms, again based on classical proportions, have been made more subtle and pleasanter. The caps are based on an alphabet used by Gill for a Bristol bookshop and are intended to be the simplest expression of the essential forms of the alphabet. It has a most comprehensive range of weights and versions, and a vast range of symbols, due to its excellence (with its very clear figures) as a timetable face. A very important face, which had a prolonged and well-justified success.

RQENbaegn

Enlarged from
30pt London Transport Johnston's Railway Type

RQENbaegn
RQENbaegn

Enlarged from
30pt Monotype 275 Gill Sans Bold and 262 Medium

ABCDEFGHIJKLMNOPQRSTUVWXYZ
abcdefghijklmnopqrstuvwxyz
&£1234567890.,;:-!?'""''/()

30pt London Transport Johnston's Railway Type

ABCDEFGHIJKLMNOPQRSTUVWXYZ
abcdefghijklmnopqrstuvwxyzæœfifffflffifl
&ÆŒ£1234567890.,;:-!?''()

ABCDEFGHIJKLMNOPQRSTUVWXYZ
abcdefghijklmnopqrstuvwxyzæœfifffflffifl
&ÆŒ£1234567890.,;:-!?''()

ABCDEFGHIJKLMNOPQRSTUVWXYZ
abcdefghijklmnopqrstuvwxyzæœfifffflffifl
&ÆŒ£1234567890.,;:-!?''()

30pt Monotype 275 Gill Sans Bold, 262 Medium and 362 Light

Futura (1927–39, Paul Renner) is the archetypal German 'geometric' sans, and perhaps the least ungainly of this rather austere species.

Spartan (1951–4) is very similar, and is the most widely used sans in the USA. Both Spartan and Futura have a complete range of weights and versions; there are numerous types by other founders which are more or less similar. Their popularity for general use is difficult to understand, though they have an unmistakable character.

Since 1816 when the Caslon foundry named their first showing of a sans 'Two line English Egyptian,' various names have been given to this family. The titles sans-serif, gothic, and grotesque, may have associations with different styles, but basically they all merely indicate serifless letters with strokes of more or less even weight.

RQENbaegn
RQENbaegn

Enlarged from
30pt Bauer Futura Bold and Medium

RQENbaegn
RQENbaegn

Enlarged from
24pt Linotype (Mergenthaler) Spartan Bold and Medium

ABCDEFGHIJKLMNOPQRSTUVWXYZ
abcdefghijklmnopqrstuvwxyzæœfffifl
&ÆŒ£1234567890.,;:-!?''()

ABCDEFGHIJKLMNOPQRSTUVWXYZ
abcdefghijklmnopqrstuvwxyzæœfffifl
&ÆŒ£1234567890.,;:-!?''()

30pt Bauer Futura Bold and Medium

ABCDEFGHIJKLMNOPQRSTUVWXYZ
abcdefghijklmnopqrstuvwxyz
&£1234567890.,;:-!?ˇ()

ABCDEFGHIJKLMNOPQRSTUVWXYZ
abcdefghijklmnopqrstuvwxyz
&$1234567890.,;:-!?ˇ()

24pt Linotype (Mergenthaler) Spartan Bold and Medium

The first three types on this spread, unlike recent grotesques, are in one weight only. *Grot 8* (1898–9, Eleisha Pechey) and *Grot 9* (1906, probably with Pechey) are both not only characteristic of English grots of the period, but also of this founder, with their tuck-ins to the c, e, r, etc. Today slightly outmoded, they have none the less an interesting character. *Grot 150* (1921), although from an earlier Miller & Richard face, is quite modern in feeling, only a few characters like F, G, and R revealing its origin ; forms which give it its own flavour. *Etrusco* is the last grotesque to exhibit, undefiled, the spirit of the nineteenth century, and bears, in its bold version, an interesting resemblance to Royal Gothic, though more regular and even in colour. *News Gothic* (1908, M. F. Benton ; bold, 1958, J. L. Renshaw) is a rather narrow form, with other, yet more condensed versions in the range. *Record* (1955–60, R. H. Middleton), with a complete range of weights and versions, is the American equivalent of the European grotesques of the next two pages, and follows the English form and the Swiss teachings of, for example, Walter Käch, of Zurich. The best European grotesques, perhaps by retaining a little more of the oddities and irregularities of the Victorian forms, seem a shade more subtle and sensitive.

Franklin (1903, M. F. Benton) is also based on English models, but is in one weight, though with different versions, only. *Eurostile* (1964–5, Aldo Novarese) is quite a different thing, and derives from the same designer's Microgramma ; but unlike that type includes lower case. All the Microgramma caps have

Enlarged from
30pt Stephenson Blake Grotesque 8

Enlarged from
30pt Stephenson Blake Grotesque 9

Enlarged from
30pt Monotype 150 Grotesque Bold Extended

Enlarged from
28D Nebiolo Etrusco Extra Bold

been designed anew for Eurostile. There is a full range of
weights and widths. The form bears a close resemblance
to a traditional Italian signwriting form (often seen in a
shadow version).

RQENbaegn
RQENbaegn

Enlarged from
30pt ATF News Gothic Bold and Medium

RQENbaegn
RQENbaegn

Enlarged from
30pt Ludlow Record Gothic Bold and Medium

RQENbaegn

Enlarged from
30pt ATF Franklin Gothic

RQENbaegn
RQENbaegn

Enlarged from
30pt Nebiolo Eurostile Bold and Medium

The types on this spread are all closely related, having common basic ancestors in nineteenth-century English or Continental forms; but while they have all been regularized to a greater or lesser degree to suit modern taste and requirements, they avoid the brutally dogmatic geometry of the Futura school. They are still designed for the eye, not for the mind. Most have a wide range of weights and versions, some (Venus, Folio, Standard, Univers) a very extensive range. *Grots 215* and *216* (1926) and *126* (1927; see alphabets) are of obscure origin. *Mercator* was designed 1957–8 by D. Dooijes;

Venus was brought out in its different weights between 1907–27.

Folio (1957–62, Konrad F. Bauer and Walter Baum) could be considered as Bauer's second thoughts on Venus, and is one of the most successful grotesque families, with a particularly good extra bold which has some resemblance to Royal Gothic. *Univers* (commenced 1952, Adrian Frutiger) is the most ambitious type series yet produced, being conceived as a completely related range (many types get different versions added as afterthoughts, while others, even Folio, fail to keep the

same character properly throughout all weights). It was originated by Deberny & Peignot, but has been designed for machine composition and film-setting too. Monotype made minor modifications for the former, but more drastic changes were necessary for Monophoto, for which one set of matrices is used for all sizes from 6 to 22pt. The face was deliberately designed to avoid nineteenth-century associations or a strong 'personality', so that it could be used unobtrusively in any situation. This aim has almost necessarily made the display sizes look weak. *Normal Grotesque* (1909–15, but some characters modified by

Enlarged from
30D on 36pt Monotype 216 Grotesque Bold and 215 Medium

Enlarged from
30pt Amsterdam Mercator Bold and Medium

Enlarged from
30pt Bauer Venus Bold and Medium

Enlarged from
30pt Bauer Folio Medium and Light

Haas 1954–5) has versions by several founders, and was originally known as Akzidenz Grotesk. *Standard* (normal 1898, light 1902, medium 1909) is also known as Akzidenz Grotesk, but is quite different from the previous type. New versions were added 1950–60. One of the best and most influential grots, the earlier normal and light weights reveal characteristic irregularities; but in 1962 *series 57* (normal) and *series 58* (smaller sizes of medium) were brought out, and are greatly improved and regularized versions (see page 105). *Helvetica* (1951, M. Miedinger) – which used to be known as New Haas Grotesque – is, in light and medium weights, probably the best and purest of them all, while retaining personality and character. Unfortunately the bold is less successful, and although condensed and expanded versions have also recently been issued, it is essentially a two-weight type; as such, it is difficult to see how it can be bettered. But the successful design of a grotesque in all sizes, combined with the perfect relationship of all weights, is a problem yet to be solved.

Enlarged from
28D on 30pt Monotype 693 Univers Bold and 689 Medium

Enlarged from
28D Haas Normal Grotesque Bold and Light

Enlarged from
30pt Berthold Standard Medium and Normal

Enlarged from
28D Haas Helvetica Medium and Light

ABCDEFGHIJKLMNOPQRSTUVWXYZ
abcdefghijklmnopqrstuvwxyz
&£1234567890.,:;-!?""'()

30pt Stephenson Blake Grotesque 8

ABCDEFGHIJKLMNOPQRSTUVWXYZ
abcdefghijklmnopqrstuvwxyz
&£1234567890.,:;-!?"

30pt Stephenson Blake Grotesque 9

ABCDEFGHIJKLMNOPQRSTUVWXYZ
abcdefghijklmnopqrstuvwxyzæœ
fiflffffiffl&ÆŒ£1234567890.,:;-!?''()

30pt Monotype 150 Grotesque Bold Extended

ABCDEFGHIJKLMNOPQRSTUVWXYZ
abcdefghijklmnopqrstuvwxyz
&1234567890.,:;'-!?()

28D Nebiolo Etrusco Extra Bold

ABCDEFGHIJKLMNOPQRSTUVWXYZ
abcdefghijklmnopqrstuvwxyz
&$1234567890.,-:;!?"
ABCDEFGHIJKLMNOPQRSTUVWXYZ
abcdefghijklmnopqrstuvwxyz
&$1234567890.,-:;!?'

30pt ATF News Gothic Bold and Medium

ABCDEFGHIJKLMNOPQRSTUVWXYZ
abcdefghijklmnopqrstuvwxyzæœ
&ÆŒ£1234567890.,:;-!?"()
ABCDEFGHIJKLMNOPQRSTUVWXYZ
abcdefghijklmnopqrstuvwxyzæœ
&ÆŒ£1234567890.,:;-!?"()

30pt Ludlow Record Gothic Bold and Medium

ABCDEFGHIJKLMNOPQRSTUVWXYZ
abcdefghijklmnopqrstuvwxyz
&$1234567890.,-:;!?'

30pt ATF Franklin Gothic

ABCDEFGHIJKLMNOPQRSTUVWXYZ
abcdefghijklmnopqrstuvwxyzæœ
&ÆŒ£1234567890.,;:-!?0

ABCDEFGHIJKLMNOPQRSTUVWXYZ
abcdefghijklmnopqrstuvwxyzæœ
&ÆŒ£1234567890.,;:-!?0

30pt Nebiolo Eurostile Bold and Medium

ABCDEFGHIJKLMNOPQRSTUVWXYZ
abcdefghijklmnopqrstuvwxyzæœ
fffiflffifffl &ÆŒ£1234567890.,;:-!?''()

ABCDEFGHIJKLMNOPQRSTUVWXYZ
abcdefghijklmnopqrstuwvxyzæœfffiflffifffl
&ÆŒ£1234567890.,;:-!?''()

ABCDEFGHIJKLMNOPQRSTUVWXYZ
abcdefghijklmnopqrstuvwxyzæœfiflfffffiffl
&ÆŒ£1234567890.,:;-!?''()

30D on 36pt Monotype 216 Grotesque Bold, 215 Medium and 126 Light

ABCDEFGHIJKLMNOPQRSTUVWXYZ
abcdefghijklmnopqrstuvwxyzæœ
&ÆŒ£1234567890.,;:-!?''()

ABCDEFGHIJKLMNOPQRSTUVWXYZ
abcdefghijklmnopqrstuvwxyz
&£1234567890.,;:-!?'')

30pt Amsterdam Mercator Bold and Medium

ABCDEFGHIJKLMNOPQRSTUVWXYZ
abcdefghijklmnopqrstuvwxyzæœ
&ÆŒ£1234567890.,;:-!?''()
ABCDEFGHIJKLMNOPQRSTUVWXYZ
abcdefghijklmnopqrstuvwxyzæœ
&ÆŒ£1234567890.,;:-!?''()

30pt Bauer Venus Bold and Medium

ABCDEFGHIJKLMNOPQRSTUVWXYZ
abcdefghijklmnopqrstuvwxyzæœ
&ÆŒ£1234567890.,;:-!?''()
ABCDEFGHIJKLMNOPQRSTUVWXYZ
abcdefghijklmnopqrstuvwxyzæœ
&ÆŒ£1234567890.,;:-!?''()
ABCDEFGHIJKLMNOPQRSTUVWXYZ
abcdefghijklmnopqrstuvwxyzæœ
&ÆŒ£1234567890.,;:-!?''()

30pt Bauer Folio Extrabold, Medium and Light

ABCDEFGHIJKLMNOPQRSTUVWXYZ
abcdefghijklmnopqrstuvwxyzæœ
&ÆŒ£1234567890.,;:-!?''()
ABCDEFGHIJKLMNOPQRSTUVWXYZ
abcdefghijklmnopqrstuvwxyzæœ
&ÆŒ£1234567890.,;:-!?''()
ABCDEFGHIJKLMNOPQRSTUVWXYZ
abcdefghijklmnopqrstuvwxyzæœ
&ÆŒ£1234567890.,;:-!?''()
ABCDEFGHIJKLMNOPQRSTUVWXYZ
abcdefghijklmnopqrstuvwxyzæœ
&ÆŒ£1234567890.,;:-!?''()

28D on 30pt Monotype 696 Univers Extrabold, 693 Bold, 689 Medium and 685 Light

ABCDEFGHIJKLMNOPQRSTUVWXYZ
abcdefghijklmnopqrstuvwxyzæœ
&ÆŒ1234567890.,;:-!?',,"()

ABCDEFGHIJKLMNOPQRSTUVWXYZ
abcdefghijklmnopqrstuvwxyzæœ
&ÆŒ1234567890.,;:-!?',,"()

28D Haas Normal Grotesque Bold and Light

ABCDEFGHIJKLMNOPQRSTUVWXYZ
abcdefghijklmnopqrstuvwxyzæœ
&ÆŒ£1234567890.,;:-!?"()

ABCDEFGHIJKLMNOPQRSTUVWXYZ
abcdefghijklmnopqrstuvwxyz
&ÆŒ£1234567890.,;:-!?"()

ABCDEFGHIJKLMNOPQRSTUVWXYZ
abcdefghijklmnopqrstuvwxyzæœ
&ÆŒ£1234567890.,;:-!?"()

30pt Berthold Standard Medium, Normal and 24pt Light

ABCDEFGHIJKLMNOPQRSTUVWXYZ
abcdefghijklmnopqrstuvwxyz
&$£1234567890.,;:?!-'

ABCDEFGHIJKLMNOPQRSTUVWXYZ
abcdefghijklmnopqrstuvwxyzæœ
&ÆŒ1234567890.,;:-!?',,"()

ABCDEFGHIJKLMNOPQRSTUVWXYZ
abcdefghijklmnopqrstuvwxyzæœ
&ÆŒ£1234567890.,;:-!?',,"()

28D Haas Helvetica Bold, Medium and Light

Settings of the text faces which appear in this atlas are shown overleaf. It is thus possible to compare the texture, colour, brilliance and legibility of each type when in use. However, to show the great variety of effects possible one would also need to compare the look of different leadings printed on different papers by several processes. The language itself might have an influence on the choice of face : Latin, for example, with its frequent q's, m's, n's and o's, looks quite different from English.

All but a few of our examples are in 10pt, variously leaded, and of equal column width. The ideal size, leading, and 'measure' is, of course, dependent upon the use to which the type is put ; each typeface requires careful individual consideration for its particular purpose. It would be also instructive to compare text settings of type of equal x-height.

Many new designs of text faces tend to be rather condensed, with short extenders, partly to save space. 'Type-designers chop the extenders short to allow the lines to be crowded together ; typographers space the lines out again to compensate for this mutilation.' The result of this is often better and more legible than allowing the extenders to control the spaces between lines. Roman inscriptions and early printing produced fine textures, but we find them hard to read. Setting unleaded grotesques in text makes the page as even and orderly as a sheet of Zip-a-tone ; and about as legible. But well-leaded grots have yet to be proved less legible than seriffed faces. The length of a line and the relationship of point size to size of printed area are equally important considerations affecting legibility.

In letterpress printing, rough paper requires a heavy impression which thickens the letter forms ; and smooth hard paper over-emphasizes the brilliance of types with strongly contrasting thick and thin strokes. This atlas is printed by offset-lithography which, owing to the thin ink used and the even contact of the offset roller with the paper, does not distort the image or thicken the forms, though the slight halation during the photographic preparation of the litho-plate can cause a soft outline.

Improved techniques, however, especially on the Continent and in America, can give results as crisp and as black as letterpress. Lack of distortion and thickening allow modern text faces to be strongly drawn and very precise, though if the offset printer chosen is likely to give only average quality, a vigorous type of even weight is best, with open counters and, if seriffed, well bracketed.

Photogravure gives half-tones the greatest delicacy and richness, but the fine screen, combined with the soft paper necessary to draw out the ink from the etched hollows in the gravure roller, tends to blur outlines, thicken strokes and break hairlines in lettering. Good results can only be obtained by restricting the choice of type to those having similar characteristics to those suitable for offset.

Throughout the centuries type form has been dependent upon what was possible to print. Better machines and smoother paper have influenced the shapes of letters as much as fashion and taste. Today, if commercial expediency alone were to dictate the development of film-setting, standards could be lowered to the level of the worst Victorian printing ; but this process has within it possibilities of refinement and subtelty beyond the skill even of the printers of the French Renaissance.

The Orient Express was stranded, with all its transient passengers, at a suburban station, on the platform of which, reflected in puddles, picturesque peasants stood and gaped at the curtained windows of the long, mysterious cars. The Palace, and its terraced gardens, and the city below the palatial hill, and the main city square, where decapitations and folk dances had already started, despite the weather – all this was at the heart of a cross whose arms terminated in Trieste, Graz, Budapest and Zagreb, as designated in *Rand McNally's Ready Reference Atlas of the World*.

10 on 11pt Monotype 252 Centaur

The Orient Express was stranded, with all its transient passengers, at a suburban station, on the platform of which, reflected in puddles, picturesque peasants stood and gaped at the curtained windows of the long, mysterious cars. The Palace, and its terraced gardens, and the city below the palatial hill, and the main city square, where decapitations and folk dances had already started, despite the weather – all this was at the heart of a cross whose arms terminated in Trieste, Graz, Budapest, and Zagreb, as designated in *Rand McNally's Ready Reference Atlas of the World*.

10 on 11pt Monotype 270 Bembo

The Orient Express was stranded, with all its transient passengers, at a suburban station, on the platform of which, reflected in puddles, picturesque peasants stood and gaped at the curtained windows of the long mysterious cars. The Palace, and its terraced gardens, and the city below the palatial hill, and the main city square, where decapitations and folk dances had already started, despite the weather – all this was at the heart of a cross whose arms terminated in Trieste, Graz, Budapest and Zagreb, as designated in *Rand McNally's Ready Reference Atlas of the World*.

10 on 12pt Monotype 170 Poliphilus and 119 Blado Italic

The Orient Express was stranded, with all its transient passengers, at a suburban station, on the platform of which, reflected in puddles, picturesque peasants stood and gaped at the curtained windows of the long, mysterious cars. The Palace, and its terraced gardens, and the city below the palatial hill, and the main city square, where decapitations and folk dances had already started, despite the weather – all this was at the heart of a cross whose arms terminated in Trieste, Graz, Budapest and Zagreb, as designated in *Rand McNally's Ready Reference Atlas of the World*.

10 on 12pt Monotype 291 Goudy Old Style

The Orient Express was stranded, with all its transient passengers, at a suburban station, on the platform of which, reflected in puddles, picturesque peasants stood and gaped at the curtained windows of the long, mysterious cars. The Palace, and its terraced gardens, and the city below the palatial hill, and the main city square, where decapitations and folk dances had already started, despite the weather – all this was at the heart of a cross whose arms terminated in Trieste, Graz, Budapest, and Zagreb, as designated in *Rand McNally's Ready Reference Atlas of the World*.

10 on 12pt Monotype 156 Garamond

The Orient Express was stranded, with all its transient passengers, at a suburban station, on the platform of which, reflected in puddles, pictur-esque peasants stood and gaped at the curtained windows of the long, mysterious cars. The Palace, and its terraced gardens, and the city below the palatial hill, and the main city square, where decapitations and folk dances had already started, despite the weather — all this was at the heart of a cross whose arms terminated in Trieste, Graz, Budapest, and Zagreb, as designated in *Rand McNally's Ready Reference Atlas of the World*.

10 on 12pt Linotype Granjon

The Orient Express was stranded, with all its transient passengers, at a suburban station, on the platform of which, reflected in puddles, picturesque peasants stood and gaped at the curtained windows of the long, mysterious cars. The Palace, and its terraced gardens, and the city below the palatial hill, and the main city square, where decapitations and folk dances had already started, despite the weather — all this was at the heart of a cross whose arms terminated in Trieste, Graz, Budapest, and Zagreb, as designated in *Rand McNally's Ready Reference Atlas of the World*.

10 on 12pt Linotype Estienne

The Orient Express was stranded, with all its transient passengers, at a suburban station, on the platform of which, reflected in puddles, picturesque peasants stood and gaped at the curtained windows of the long, mysterious cars. The Palace, and its terraced gardens, and the city below the palatial hill, and the main city square, where decapitations and folk dances had already started, despite the weath-er – all this was at the heart of a cross whose arms terminated in Trieste, Graz, Budapest, and Zagreb, as designated in *Rand McNally's Ready Reference Atlas of the World*.

10 on 12pt Monotype 2 Old Style No 2

The Orient Express was stranded, with all its transient passengers, at a suburban station, on the platform of which, reflected in puddles, pictur-esque peasants stood and gaped at the curtained windows of the long, mysterious cars. The Palace, and its terraced gardens, and the city below the palatial hill, and the main city square, where decapitations and folk dances had already started, despite the weather – all this was at the heart of a cross whose arms terminated in Trieste, Graz, Budapest, and Zagreb, as designated in *Rand McNally's Ready Reference Atlas of the World*.

10 on 13pt Monotype 110 Plantin

The Orient Express was stranded, with all its transient passengers, at a suburban station, on the platform of which, reflected in puddles, picturesque peasants stood and gaped at the curtained windows of the long, mysterious cars. The Palace, and its terraced gardens, and the city below the palatial hill, and the main city square, where decapitations and folk dances had already started, despite the weather – all this was at the heart of a cross whose arms terminated in Trieste, Graz, Budapest and Zagreb, as designated in *Rand McNally's Ready Reference Atlas of the World*.

10 on 12pt Monotype 203 Van Dijck

The Orient Express was stranded, with all its transient passengers, at a suburban station, on the platform of which, reflected in puddles, picturesque peasants stood and gaped at the curtained windows of the long, mysterious cars. The Palace, and its terraced gardens, and the city below the palatial hill, and the main city square, where decapitations and folk dances had already started, despite the weather — all this was at the heart of a cross whose arms terminated in Trieste, Graz, Budapest, and Zagreb, as designated in *Rand McNally's Ready Reference Atlas of the World*.

10 on 12pt Linotype Janson

The Orient Express was stranded, with all its transient passengers, at a suburban station, on the platform of which, reflected in puddles, pictur-esque peasants stood and gaped at the curtained windows of the long, mysterious cars. The Palace, and its terraced gardens, and the city below the palatial hill, and the main city square, where decapitations and folk dances had already started, despite the weather – all this was at the heart of a cross whose arms terminated in Trieste, Graz, Budapest and Zagreb, as designated in *Rand McNally's Ready Reference Atlas of the World*.

10 on 13pt Monotype 453 Ehrhardt

The Orient Express was stranded, with all its transient passengers, at a sub-urban station, on the platform of which, reflected in puddles, picturesque peasants stooed and gaped at the curtained windows of the long, mysterious cars. The Palace, and its terraced gardens, and the city below the palatial hill, and the main city square, where decapitations and folk dances had already started, despite the weather – all this was at the heart of a cross whose arms terminated in Trieste, Graz, Budapest, and Zagreb, as designated in *Rand McNally's Ready Reference Atlas of the World*.

10 on 12pt Monotype 128 Caslon

The Orient Express was stranded, with all its transient passengers, at a sub-urban station, on the platform of which, reflected in puddles, picturesque peas-ants stood and gaped at the curtained windows of the long, mysterious cars. The Palace, and its terraced gardens, and the city below the palatial hill, and the main city square, where decapitations and folk dances had already started, despite the weather—all this was at the heart of a cross whose arms terminated in Trieste, Graz, Budapest, and Zagreb, as designated in *Rand McNally's Ready Reference Atlas of the World*.

10 on 12pt Linotype Caslon

The Orient Express was stranded, with all its transient passengers, at a suburban station, on the platform of which, reflected in puddles, picturesque peasants stood and gaped at the curtained windows of the long, mysterious cars. The Palace, and its terraced gardens, and the city below the palatial hill, and the main city square, where decapitations and folk dances had already started, despite the weather – all this was at the heart of a cross whose arms terminated in Trieste, Graz, Budapest, and Zagreb, as designated in *Rand McNally's Ready Reference Atlas of the World*.

10 on 12pt Monotype 101 Imprint

The Orient Express was stranded, with all its transient passengers, at a suburban station, on the platform of which, reflected in puddles, picturesque peasants stood and gaped at the curtained windows of the long, mysterious cars. The Palace, and its terraced gardens, and the city below the palatial hill, and the main city square, where decapitations and folk dances had already started, despite the weather – all this was at the heart of a cross whose arms terminated in Trieste, Graz, Budapest and Zagreb, as designated in *Rand McNally's Ready Reference Atlas of the World.*
10 on 12pt Monotype 185 Fournier

The Orient Express was stranded, with all its transient passengers, at a suburban station, on the platform of which, reflected in puddles, picturesque peasants stood and gaped at the curtained windows of the long, mysterious cars. The Palace, and its terraced gardens, and the city below the palatial hill, and the main city square, where decapitations and folk dances had already started, despite the weather – all this was at the heart of a cross whose arms terminated in Trieste, Graz, Budapest, and Zagreb, as designated in *Rand McNally's Ready Reference Atlas of the World.*
10 on 12pt Monotype 169 Baskerville

The Orient Express was stranded, with all its transient passengers, at a suburban station, on the platform of which, reflected in puddles, picturesque peasants stood and gaped at the curtained windows of the long, mysterious cars. The Palace, and its terraced gardens, and the city below the palatial hill, and the main city square, where decapitations and folk dances had already started, despite the weather — all this was at the heart of a cross whose arms terminated in Trieste, Graz, Budapest, and Zagreb, as designated in *Rand McNally's Ready Reference Atlas of the World.*
10 on 12pt Linotype Baskerville

The Orient Express was stranded, with all its transient passengers, at a suburban station, on the platform of which, reflected in puddles, picturesque peasants stood and gaped at the curtained windows of the long, mysterious cars. The Palace, and its terraced gardens, and the city below the palatial hill, and the main city square, where decapitations and folk dances had already started, despite the weather — all this was at the heart of a cross whose arms terminated in Trieste, Graz, Budapest, and Zagreb, as designated in *Rand McNally's Ready Reference Atlas of the World.*
10 on 12pt Linotype Georgian

The Orient Express was stranded, with all its transient passengers, at a suburban station, on the platform of which, reflected in puddles, picturesque peasants stood and gaped at the curtained windows of the long, mysterious cars. The Palace, and its terraced gardens, and the city below the palatial hill, and the main city square, where decapitations and folk dances had already started, despite the weather – all this was at the heart of a cross whose arms terminated in Trieste, Graz, Budapest and Zagreb, as designated in *Rand McNally's Ready Reference Atlas of the World.*
10 on 13pt Monotype 403 Fontana

The Orient Express was stranded, with all its transient passengers, at a suburban station, on the platform of which, reflected in puddles, picturesque peasants stood and gaped at the curtained windows of the long, mysterious cars. The Palace, and its terraced gardens, and the city below the palatial hill, and the main city square, where decapitations and folk dances had already started, despite the weather – all this was at the heart of a cross whose arms terminated in Trieste, Graz, Budapest and Zagreb, as designated in *Rand McNally's Ready Reference Atlas of the World.*
10 on 12pt Monotype 341 Bell

The Orient Express was stranded, with all its transient passengers, at a suburban station, on the platform of which, reflected in puddles, picturesque peasants stood and gaped at the curtained windows of the long, mysterious cars. The Palace, and its terraced gardens, and the city below the palatial hill, and the main city square, where decapitations and folk dances had already started, despite the weather – all this was at the heart of a cross whose arms terminated in Trieste, Graz, Budapest and Zagreb, as designated in *Rand McNally's Ready Reference Atlas of the World.*
11 on 13pt Monotype 469 Bulmer

The Orient Express was stranded, with all its transient passengers, at a suburban station, on the platform of which, reflected in puddles, picturesque peasants stood and gaped at the curtained windows of the long, mysterious cars. The Palace, and its terraced gardens, and the city below the palatial hill, and the main city square, where decapitations and folk dances had already started, despite the weather – all this was at the heart of a cross whose arms terminated in Trieste, Graz, Budapest and Zagreb, as designated in *Rand McNally's Ready Reference Atlas of the World.*
10 on 13pt Monotype 46 Scotch Roman

The Orient Express was stranded, with all its transient passengers, at a suburban station, on the platform of which, reflected in puddles, picturesque peasants stood and gaped at the curtained windows of the long, mysterious cars. The Palace, and its terraced gardens, and the city below the palatial hill, and the main city square, where decapitations and folk dances had already started, despite the weather — all this was at the heart of a cross whose arms terminated in Trieste, Graz, Budapest, and Zagreb, as designated in *Rand McNally's Ready Reference Atlas of the World.*
10 on 13pt Linotype Scotch Roman 2

The Orient Express was stranded, with all its transient passengers, at a suburban station, on the platform of which, reflected in puddles, picturesque peasants stood and gaped at the curtained windows of the long, mysterious cars. The Palace, and its terraced gardens, and the city below the palatial hill, and the main city square, where decapitations and folk dances had already started, despite the weather – all this was at the heart of a cross whose arms terminated in Trieste, Graz, Budapest and Zagreb, as designated in *Rand McNally's Ready Reference Atlas of the World.*
10 on 13pt Monotype 71 Didot

The Orient Express was stranded, with all its transient passengers, at a suburban station, on the platform of which, reflected in puddles, picturesque peasants stood and gaped at the curtained windows of the long, mysterious cars. The Palace, and its terraced gardens, and the city below the palatial hill, and the main city square, where decapitations and folk dances had already started, despite the weather – all this was at the heart of a cross whose arms terminated in Trieste, Graz, Budapest, and Zagreb, as designated in *Rand McNally's Ready Reference Atlas of the World.*
10 on 12pt Monotype 374 Walbaum

The Orient Express was stranded, with all its transient passengers, at a suburban station, on the platform of which, reflected in puddles, picturesque peasants stood and gaped at the curtained windows of the long, mysterious cars. The Palace, and its terraced gardens, and the city below the palatial hill, and the main city square, where decapitations and folk dances had already started, despite the weather – all this was at the heart of a cross whose arms terminated in Trieste, Graz, Budapest, and Zagreb, as designated in *Rand McNally's Ready Reference Atlas of the World.*
10 on 13pt Monotype 135 Bodoni

The Orient Express was stranded, with all its transient passengers, at a suburban station, on the platform of which, reflected in puddles, picturesque peasants stood and gaped at the curtained windows of the long, mysterious cars. The Palace, and its terraced gardens, and the city below the palatial hill, and the main city square, where decapitations and folk dances had already started, despite the weather – all this was at the heart of a cross whose arms terminated in Trieste, Graz, Budapest and Zagreb, as designated in *Rand McNally's Ready Reference Atlas of the World.*
10 on 13pt Monotype 357 Bodoni Book

The Orient Express was stranded, with all its transient passengers, at a suburban station, on the platform of which, reflected in puddles, picturesque peasants stood and gaped at the curtained windows of the long, mysterious cars. The Palace, and its terraced gardens, and the city below the palatial hill, and the main city square, where decapitations and folk dances had already started, despite the weather – all this was at the heart of a cross whose arms terminated in Trieste, Graz, Budapest, and Zagreb, as designated in *Rand McNally's Ready Reference Atlas of the World.*
10 on 13pt Monotype 7 Modern Extended

The Orient Express was stranded, with all its transient passengers, at a suburban station, on the platform of which, reflected in puddles, picturesque peasants stood and gaped at the curtained windows of the long, mysterious cars. The Palace, and its terraced gardens, and the city below the palatial hill, and the main city square, where decapitations and folk dances had already started, despite the weather – all this was at the heart of a cross whose arms terminated in Trieste, Graz, Budapest and Zagreb, as designated in *Rand McNally's Ready Reference Atlas of the World*.

9 on 14pt Monotype 342 Ionic

The Orient Express was stranded, with all its transient passengers, at a suburban station, on the platform of which, reflected in puddles, picturesque peasants stood and gaped at the curtained windows of the long, mysterious cars. The Palace, and its terraced gardens, and the city below the palatial hill, and the main city square, where decapitations and folk dances had already started, despite the weather – all this was at the heart of a cross whose arms terminated in Trieste, Graz, Budapest and Zagreb, as designated in *Rand McNally's Ready Reference Atlas of the World*.

10 on 14pt Monotype 227 Century

The Orient Express was stranded, with all its transient passengers, at a suburban station, on the platform of which, reflected in puddles, picturesque peasants stood and gaped at the curtained windows of the long, mysterious cars. The Palace, and its terraced gardens, and the city below the palatial hill, and the main city square, where decapitations and folk dances had already started, despite the weather – all this was at the heart of a cross whose arms terminated in Trieste, Graz, Budapest and Zagreb, as designated in *Rand McNally's Ready Reference Atlas of the World*.

10 on 11pt Monotype 239 Perpetua

The Orient Express was stranded, with all its transient passengers, at a suburban station, on the platform of which, reflected in puddles, picturesque peasants stood and gaped at the curtained windows of the long, mysterious cars. The Palace, and its terraced gardens, and the city below the palatial hill, and the main city square, where decapitations and folk dances had already started, despite the weather – all this was at the heart of a cross whose arms terminated in Trieste, Graz, Budapest and Zagreb, as designated in *Rand McNally's Ready Reference Atlas of the World*.

10 on 12pt Monotype 478 Joanna

The Orient Express was stranded, with all its transient passengers, at a suburban station, on the platform of which, reflected in puddles, picturesque peasants stood and gaped at the curtained windows of the long, mysterious cars. The Palace, and its terraced gardens, and the city below the palatial hill, and the main city square, where decapitations and folk dances had already started, despite the weather—all this was at the heart of a cross whose arms terminated in Trieste, Graz, Budapest, and Zagreb, as designated in *Rand McNally's Ready Reference Atlas of the World*.

10 on 12pt Linotype Pilgrim

The Orient Express was stranded, with all its transient passengers, at a suburban station, on the platform of which, reflected in puddles, picturesque peasants stood and gaped at the curtained windows of the long, mysterious cars. The Palace, and its terraced gardens, and the city below the palatial hill, and the main city square, where decapitations and folk dances had already started, despite the weather – all this was at the heart of a cross whose arms terminated in Trieste, Graz, Budapest and Zagreb, as designated in *Rand McNally's Ready Reference Atlas of the World*.

10 on 11pt Monotype 320 Emerson

The Orient Express was stranded, with all its transient passengers, at a suburban station, on the platform of which, reflected in puddles, picturesque peasants stood and gaped at the curtained windows of the long, mysterious cars. The Palace, and its terraced gardens, and the city below the palatial hill, and the main city square, where decapitations and folk dances had already started, despite the weather – all this was at the heart of a cross whose arms terminated in Trieste, Graz, Budapest and Zagreb, as designated in *Rand McNally's Ready Reference Atlas of the World*.

10D on 13pt Monotype 255 Lutetia

The Orient Express was stranded, with all its transient passengers, at a suburban station, on the platform of which, reflected in puddles, picturesque peasants stood and gaped at the curtained windows of the long, mysterious cars. The Palace, and its terraced gardens, and the city below the palatial hill, and the main city square, where decapitations and folk dances had already started, despite the weather – all this was at the heart of a cross whose arms terminated in Trieste, Graz, Budapest and Zagreb, as designated in *Rand McNally's Ready Reference Atlas of the World*.

10D on 13pt Monotype 556 Spectrum

The Orient Express was stranded, with all its transient passengers, at a suburban station, on the platform of which, reflected in puddles, picturesque peasants stood and gaped at the curtained windows of the long, mysterious cars. The Palace, and its terraced gardens, and the city below the palatial hill, and the main city square, where decapitations and folk dances had already started, despite the weather – all this was at the heart of a cross whose arms terminated in Trieste, Graz, Budapest and Zagreb, as designated in *Rand McNally's Ready Reference Atlas of the World*.

10D on 12pt Monotype 592 Dante

The Orient Express was stranded, with all its transient passengers, at a suburban station, on the platform of which, reflected in puddles, picturesque peasants stood and gaped at the curtained windows of the long, mysterious cars. The Palace, and its terraced gardens, and the city below the palatial hill, and the main city square, where decapitations and folk dances had already started, despite the weather — all this was at the heart of a cross whose arms terminated in Trieste, Graz, Budapest, and Zagreb, as designated in *Rand McNally's Ready Reference Atlas of the World*.

10 on 11pt Linotype Electra

The Orient Express was stranded, with all its transient passengers, at a suburban station, on the platform of which, reflected in puddles, picturesque peasants stood and gaped at the curtained windows of the long, mysterious cars. The Palace, and its terraced gardens, and the city below the palatial hill, and the main city square, where decapitations and folk dances had already started, despite the weather — all this was at the heart of a cross whose arms terminated in Trieste, Graz, Budapest, and Zagreb, as designated in *Rand McNally's Ready Reference Atlas of the World*.

10 on 11pt Linotype Caledonia

The Orient Express was stranded, with all its transient passengers, at a suburban station, on the platform of which, reflected in puddles, picturesque peasants stood and gaped at the curtained windows of the long, mysterious cars. The Palace, and its terraced gardens, and the city below the palatial hill, and the main city square, where decapitations and folk dances had already started, despite the weather —all this was at the heart of a cross whose arms terminated in Trieste, Graz, Budapest, and Zagreb, as designated in *Rand McNally's Ready Reference Atlas of the World*.

10 on 11pt Linotype Juliana

The Orient Express was stranded, with all its transient passengers, at a suburban station, on the platform of which, reflected in puddles, picturesque peasants stood and gaped at the curtained windows of the long, mysterious cars. The Palace, and its terraced gardens, and the city below the palatial hill, and the main city square, where decapitations and folk dances had already started, despite the weather — all this was at the heart of a cross whose arms terminated in Trieste, Graz, Budapest, and Zagreb, as designated in *Rand McNally's Ready Reference Atlas of the World*.

10 on 13pt Linotype Melior

The Orient Express was stranded, with all its transient passengers, at a suburban station, on the platform of which, reflected in puddles, picturesque peasants stood and gaped at the curtained windows of the long, mysterious cars. The Palace, and its terraced gardens, and the city below the palatial hill, and the main city square, where decapitations and folk dances had already started, despite the weather — all this was at the heart of a cross whose arms terminated in Trieste, Graz, Budapest, and Zagreb, as designated in *Rand McNally's Ready Reference Atlas of the World*.

10 on 13pt Linotype Aldus

The Orient Express was stranded, with all its transient passengers, at a suburban station, on the platform of which, reflected in puddles, picturesque peasants stood and gaped at the curtained windows of the long, mysterious cars. The Palace, and its terraced gardens, and the city below the palatial hill, and the main city square, where decapitations and folk dances had already started, despite the weather – all this was at the heart of a cross whose arms terminated in Trieste, Graz, Budapest and Zagreb, as designated in *Rand McNally's Ready Reference Atlas of the World.*

10D on 12pt Monotype 458 Romulus

The Orient Express was stranded, with all its transient passengers, at a suburban station, on the platform of which, reflected in puddles, picturesque peasants stood and gaped at the curtained windows of the long mysterious cars. The Palace, and its terraced gardens, and the city below the palatial hill, and the main city square where decapitations and folk dances had already started, despite the weather – all this was at the heart of a cross whose arms terminated in Trieste, Graz, Budapest, and Zagreb, as designated in *Rand McNally's Ready Reference Atlas of the World.*

10 on 12pt Monotype 327 Times

The Orient Express was stranded, with all its transient passengers, at a suburban station, on the platform of which, reflected in puddles, picturesque peasants stood and gaped at the curtained windows of the long, mysterious cars. The Palace, and its terraced gardens, and the city below the palatial hill, and the main city square, where decapitations and folk dances had already started, despite the weather – all this was at the heart of a cross whose arms terminated in Trieste, Graz, Budapest and Zagreb, as designated in *Rand McNally's Ready Reference Atlas of the World.*

10 on 13pt Monotype 262 Gill Sans

The Orient Express was stranded, with all its transient passengers, at a suburban station, on the platform of which, reflected in puddles, picturesque peasants stood and gaped at the curtained windows of the long, mysterious cars. The Palace, and its terraced gardens, and the city below the palatial hill, and the main city square, where decapitations and folk dances had already started, despite the weather – all this was at the heart of a cross whose arms terminated in Trieste, Graz, Budapest, and Zagreb, as designated *in Rand McNally's Ready Reference Atlas of the World*.
10 on 13pt Monotype 362 Gill Sans Light

The Orient Express was stranded, with all its transient passengers, at a suburban station, on the platform of which, reflected in puddles, picturesque peasants stood and gaped at the curtained windows of the long, mysterious cars. The palace, and its terraced gardens, and the city below the palatial hill, and the main city square, where decapitations and folk dances had already started despite the weather — all this was at the heart of a cross whose arms terminated in Trieste, Graz, Budapest, and Zagreb, as designated in *Rand McNally's Ready Reference Atlas of the World*.
9 on 13pt Intertype Futura Book

The Orient Express was stranded, with all its transient passengers, at a suburban station, on the platform of which, reflected in puddles, picturesque peasants stood and gaped at the curtained windows of the long, mysterious cars. The Palace, and its terraced gardens, and the city below the palatial hill, and the main city square, where decapitations and folk dances had already started, despite the weather — all this was at the heart of a cross whose arms terminated in Trieste, Graz, Budapest, and Zagreb, as designated in *Rand McNally's Ready Reference Atlas of the World*.
10 on 13pt Linotype Spartan Book

The Orient Express was stranded, with all its transient passengers, at a suburban station, on the platform of which, reflected in puddles, picturesque peasants stood and gaped at the curtained windows of the long, mysterious cars. The Palace, and its terraced gardens, and the city below the palatial hill, and the main city square, where decapitations and folk dances had already started, despite the weather – all this was at the heart of a cross whose arms terminated in Trieste, Graz, Budapest, and Zagreb, as designated in *Rand McNally's Ready Reference Atlas of the World*.
9D on 13pt Monotype 215 Grotesque

The Orient Express was stranded, with all its transient passengers, at a suburban station, on the platform of which, reflected in puddles, picturesque peasants stood and gaped at the curtained windows of the long, mysterious cars. The Palace, and its terraced gardens, and the city below the palatial hill, and the main city square, where decapitations and folk dances had already started, despite the weather – all this was at the heart of a cross whose arms terminated in Trieste, Graz, Budapest and Zagreb, as designated in *Rand McNally's Ready Reference Atlas of the World*.
9D on 13pt Monotype 126 Grotesque

The Orient Express was stranded, with all its transient passengers, at a suburban station, on the platform of which, reflected in puddles, picturesque peasants stood and gaped at the curtained windows of the long, mysterious cars. The Palace, and its terraced gardens, and the city below the palatial hill, and the main city square, where decapitations and folk dances had already started, despite the weather — all this was at the heart of a cross whose arms terminated in Trieste, Graz, Budapest, and Zagreb, as designated in *Rand McNally's Ready Reference Atlas of the World*.
9 on 13pt Intertype Folio Light

The Orient Express was stranded, with all its transient passengers, at a suburban station, on the platform of which, reflected in puddles, picturesque peasants stood and gaped at the curtained windows of the long, mysterious cars. The Palace, and its terraced gardens, and the city below the palatial hill, and the main city square, where decapitations and folk dances had already started, despite the weather – all this was at the heart of a cross whose arms terminated in Trieste, Graz, Budapest, and Zagreb, as designated in *Rand McNally's Ready Reference Atlas of the World*.
9D on 13pt Monotype 689 Univers Medium

The Orient Express was stranded, with all its transient passengers, at a suburban station, on the platform of which, reflected in puddles, picturesque peasants stood and gaped at the curtained windows of the long, mysterious cars. The Palace, and its terraced gardens, and the city below the palatial hill, and the main city square, where decapitations and folk dances had already started, despite the weather – all this was at the heart of a cross whose arms terminated in Trieste, Graz, Budapest, and Zagreb, as designated in *Rand McNally's Ready Reference Atlas of the World*.
9D on 13pt Monotype 685 Univers Light

The Orient Express was stranded, with all its transient passengers, at a suburban station, on the platform of which, reflected in puddles, picturesque peasants stood and gaped at the curtained windows of the long, mysterious cars. The Palace, and its terraced gardens, and the city below the palatial hill, and the main city square, where decapitations and folk dances had already started, despite the weather —all this was at the heart of a cross whose arms terminated in Trieste, Graz, Budapest, and Zagreb, as designated in *Rand McNally's Ready Reference Atlas of the World*.
10 on 13pt Linotype Standard

The Orient Express was stranded, with all its transient passengers, at a suburban station, on the platform of which, reflected in puddles, picturesque peasants stood and gaped at the curtained windows of the long, mysterious cars. The Palace, and its terraced gardens, and the city below the palatial hill, and the main city square, where decapitations and folk dances had already started, despite the weather — all this was at the heart of a cross whose arms terminated in Trieste, Graz, Budapest, and Zagreb, as designated in *Rand McNally's Ready Reference Atlas of the World*.
10 on 13pt Linotype Helvetica

Short bibliography

Type

Encyclopaedia of Typefaces. Berry, Johnson & Jaspert. Blandford, London 1962
A Book of Type and Design. O. Hlavsa. Nevil, London 1960
Type Designs. R. Hostettler. Zollikofer, St Gall 1949
A Treasury of Alphabets and Lettering. J. Tschichold. Rheinhold, New York 1966
Hoffmanns Schriftatlas. A. Finsterer. Hoffmann, Stuttgart 1952

History

Printing Types. D. B. Updike. Oxford University Press, London 1937
Four Centuries of Fine Printing. S. Morison. Benn, London 1960
On Type Designs. S. Morison. Benn, London 1962
Type Designs. A. F. Johnson. Deutsch, London 1966
Five Hundred Years of Printing. S. H. Steinberg. Penguin, Harmondsworth 1962
Printed Books. T. M. MacRobert. HMSO, London 1957
An Introduction to the History of Printing Types. G. Dowding. Wace, London 1961
Printing and the Mind of Man. F. W. Bridges & Sons, London 1963
Vincent Figgins Type Specimens. B. Wolpe. Printing Historical Society, London 1967
Nineteenth-century Ornamented Types and Ornaments. N. Gray. Faber, London 1938
Lettering on Buildings. N. Gray. Architectural Press, London 1960

Script

A Book of Scripts. A. Fairbank. Penguin, Harmondsworth 1960
The Development of Writing. H. E. Meyer. Graphis, Zürich 1964
A Handwriting Manual. A. Fairbank. Faber, London 1954

Typography and Printing

Introduction to Typography. O. Simon. Faber, London 1963
Typography : Basic Principles. J. Lewis. Studio Vista, London 1963
The Western Typebook. Western Printing Services. Hamish Hamilton, London 1960
Methods of Book Design. H. Williamson. Oxford University Press. London 1956
The Printer's Terms. R. Hostettler. Redman, London 1963
Finer Points in the Spacing and Arrangement of Type. G. Dowding. Wace, London 1954
Factors in the Choice of Type Faces. G. Dowding. Wace, London 1957